Heroes of American History

The Leaders, Thinkers, and Revolutionaries

Publications International, Ltd.

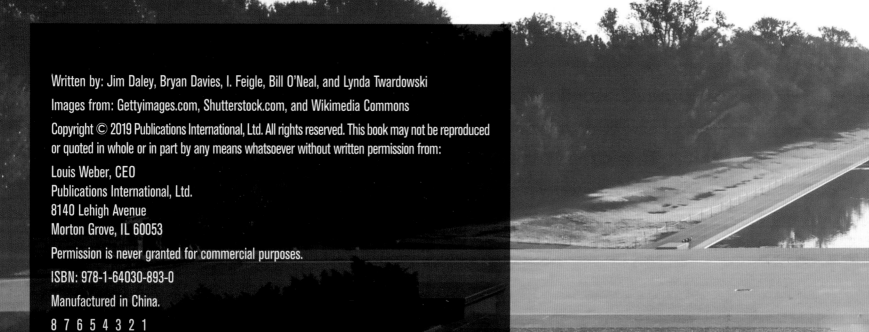

Written by: Jim Daley, Bryan Davies, I. Feigle, Bill O'Neal, and Lynda Twardowski

Images from: Gettyimages.com, Shutterstock.com, and Wikimedia Commons

Louis Weber, CEO
Publications International, Ltd.
8140 Lehigh Avenue
Morton Grove, IL 60053

Permission is never granted for commercial purposes.

ISBN: 978-1-64030-893-0

Manufactured in China.

8 7 6 5 4 3 2 1

Table of Contents

America: Home of the Brave

Top: George Washington Carver was a scientist and environmentalist who developed techniques to restore soil quality and trained farmers in the South to grow new crops.

Left: A. Philip Randolph organized the March on Washington for Jobs and Freedom in 1963, promoting the livelihood of African Americans throughout the nation.

The word "hero" has many meanings. A hero can be someone who risks their life to save others. A hero can be the person who donates their time and energy to helping those in need by starting a charity or organization. Sometimes heroes are those who stand up to hatred or intolerance. Sometimes they stand up for what is right no matter what negative repercussions they might endure. Most important, though, a hero is someone we can all look up to.

In this book, we share the stories of real-life heroes. Some names may be familiar—like Meriwether Lewis, Geronimo, Malcolm X, or Helen Keller. A hero doesn't necessarily have to risk their life in war or battle, but heroes are often willing to sacrifice everything—including their autonomy and freedom—to ensure equal opportunities are provided to others. The heroes documented in this book are part of United States history, shaping our nation from the fledgling democracy after the American Revolution to the industrial and technological booms of the twentieth century.

Top: Sidney Hillman led the Amalgamated Clothing Workers of American and was a founding of the Congress of Industrial Workers, a federation that organized steel, automobile, and textile unions under one organization.

Left: Mary Edwards Walker was an abolitionist and women's rights advocate who served as a surgeon during the Civil War. She was the first woman to receive the Medal of Honor for her efforts in the war.

Heroes of American History   5

Frederick Douglass 1818–1895

Frederick Augustus Washington Bailey, who later became internationally renowned as Frederick Douglass, was born the son of a slave mother and an unknown white father in Maryland. Trained as a shipwright (and having secretly learned how to read), young Frederick Bailey made a daring escape to freedom in 1838 and eventually ended up in Massachusetts. He took the name Douglass to reduce his chances of being identified as an escaped slave and returned to his master in Maryland.

Soon after, he met abolitionist William Lloyd Garrison, who hired him to lecture for his Anti-Slavery Society. Like his new friend and mentor, Douglass attacked the institution of slavery in the most vehement terms: "I assert most unhesitatingly that the religion of the South is a mere covering for the most horrid crimes—a justifier of the most appalling barbarity, a sanctifier of the most hateful frauds, and a dark shelter under which the darkest, foulest, grossest, and most infernal deeds of slaveholders find the strongest protection."

Douglass achieved national prominence with the 1845 publication of his first book, *Narrative of the Life of Frederick Douglass, an American Slave*. Immediately fearing arrest and re-enslavement, he went to Great Britain for two years, traveling throughout England, Ireland, and Scotland. As might be expected, the fiery Douglass exerted some of his greatest influence on the struggle against slavery during the war, urging abolition no longer simply on moral grounds but as a means of taking a critical strategic asset from the rebellious South. He also campaigned for the federal government to allow blacks to serve as soldiers. In both of these efforts, he was ultimately successful.

Frederick Douglass was known to engage in dialogue with those who were opposed to his own viewpoints, including slaveholders. Many abolitionists of the day lived by the motto, "No union with slaveholders," but Frederick Douglass famously replied to this staunch approach by declaring "I would unite with anybody to do right and nobody to do wrong."

Douglass first met abolitionist William Lloyd Garrison in New Bedford, Massachusetts, in 1841 at a meeting of the Bristol Anti-Slavery Society.

A photo of Douglass with his second wife Helen Pitts (sitting) and her sister.

After the war, Douglass did not cease his activism but in fact added the duties of a public official. Throughout the years, he served as U.S. marshal and recorder of deeds for the District of Columbia, U.S. minister to Haiti, and *chargé d'affaires* to Saint Domingue. He published two more books and several essays. After marrying Helen Pitts in 1884—she was a white feminist 20 years his junior, which caused quite the scandal at the time—Douglass also aligned himself with feminist causes and spent his later days traveling extensively throughout Europe. He finally retired to his home in Washington, D.C., where he died at age 77—or 79, depending on how you count it.

Dr. Martin Luther King Jr. 1929–1968

King was born on January 15, 1929, in Atlanta, Georgia, the son of the Rev. Martin Luther King Sr. A gifted student, he entered Morehouse College when he was just 15, and he graduated in 1948 with a Bachelor's degree in sociology. He then enrolled in Crozer Theological Seminary in Chester, Pennsylvania, graduating in 1951 with a Bachelor's degree in divinity. In addition, King earned a Doctorate's degree in philosophy from Boston University.

King became pastor of the Dexter Avenue Baptist Church in Montgomery, Alabama, in 1954. By then, he had become deeply involved in the cause for civil rights for African Americans, and in 1955 he led the Montgomery Bus Boycott, which lasted 382 days. During that time, King was arrested, his home was bombed, and he was subjected to tremendous personal abuse. But as a result of that protest, the United States Supreme Court declared all laws requiring segregation on buses unconstitutional. For the first time in history, blacks and whites could ride municipal buses as equals. The Montgomery Bus Boycott placed King in the national spotlight and established him as a leading spokesman in the fight for civil rights.

King suffered greatly in his fight for civil rights, especially in the South. He was arrested more than 20 times, assaulted at least four times, and the subject of several bomb threats. Those who followed him in the protests that he organized were often assaulted with fire hoses or set upon by police dogs. But King refused to give up, and as a result of his efforts, he was named Man of the Year by *Time* magazine in 1963. A year later, he was awarded the Nobel Prize in Peace, the youngest man ever to receive the prize. Upon learning of the honor, King announced that he would donate the $54,123 prize money to help advance the civil rights movement.

Since his death, Martin Luther King has become a cultural and social icon, and there are numerous memorials dedicated to him throughout the United States.

A law making King's birthday a federal holiday was signed by President Ronald Reagan in 1983, and the holiday—observed on the third Monday in January—was first observed by a majority of states in 1986.

King worked tirelessly to ensure equal rights for all. He promoted voter registration drives for African Americans in Alabama and directed the March on Washington for Jobs and Freedom, that drew a quarter of a million people. It was during that event, on the steps of the Lincoln Memorial, that King delivered his famous "I Have a Dream" speech (pictured here), in which he passionately advocated for racial equality and the end of discrimination.

On the evening of April 4, 1968, King was standing on a second-floor balcony at the Lorraine Motel in Memphis, Tennessee, where he was to lead a protest march on behalf of striking garbage workers, when he was felled by an assassin's bullet. James Earl Ray pleaded guilty to King's murder and was sentenced to 99 years in prison, though he later recanted his confession and spent the rest of his life claiming King's death was part of a conspiracy.

Shirley Chisholm 1924–2005

Shirley Chisholm was born Shirley Anita St. Hill in Brooklyn, New York, on November 30, 1924, to two Caribbean immigrants who had individually immigrated from Barbados to New York a few years before Shirley was born. Both parents struggled to find and keep work in the U.S., which led Shirley and her three younger sisters to be sent to Barbados to be raised by their maternal grandmother. She attended a one-room school in Barbados through her youth until she returned to New York in 1934. She was a highly regarded student at Girl's High School in Brooklyn and received a Bachelor of Arts from Brooklyn College in 1946, where she received prizes for her public speaking skills.

After graduating, she became an educator in Manhattan and Brooklyn, where she became an authority on early education and child welfare. It was during her time as an educator that she began her political career, volunteering her time in what she saw as white-dominated political parties. She served on various New York legislatures between 1965 and 1968, where she successfully attained unemployment benefits for domestic workers and helped disadvantaged students enter college while receiving remedial education. In 1968, Chisholm won the newly redrawn 12th congressional district of New York, which was established to better represent the constituents found in the Bedford-Stuyvesant neighborhood of Brooklyn. Upset by her seemingly unfitting appointment to the House Agriculture Committee, Shirley used her position to refocus surplus food into poorer and in-need communities. She would also play a pivotal role in establishing the Special Supplemental Nutrition Program for Women, Infants, and Children (WIC). Throughout her career as a congresswoman, Chisholm unabashedly supported inner-city residents and their access to social services. She also supported spending increases on education, health care, and other services while condemning increased spending on military efforts.

Chisholm was nominated to be the United States Ambassador to Jamaica in 1991 by Bill Clinton, but she had to turn the offer down because of poor health. That same year, she was inducted into the National Women's Hall of Fame.

Chisholm made a run for the presidency in 1972, but her bid for the election was largely ignored by her fellow Democrats, who saw the bid more as a symbolic action than a serious endeavor. She served in Congress until 1983 when she grew disillusioned with the Democratic party after the election of Ronald Reagan. After her time in Congress, she continued her work in education by holding the Purington Chair at Mount Holyoke College where she taught in various departments. She gave speeches throughout the rest of her life where she told young students to embrace each other's differences and to avoid intolerance. She died on New Year's Day in 2005 in Florida.

Top: Chisholm was also a founding member of the Congressional Black Caucus in 1971.

Bottom: Chisholm was vehemently opposed to the draft, America's involvement in Vietnam, and the development of military weapons.

Heroes of American History   11

Mary Edwards Walker 1832–1919

Born as the youngest of seven children to Alvah and Vesta Walker in Oswego, New York, on November 26, 1832, Mary Edwards Walker was raised in a very progressive manner for the time. Although both of her parents were Christians, they often told her to question authoritative claims and restrictions that were unfairly promoted by various Christian denominations. Her parents also broke many gender roles of the time by sharing work around the farm and not requiring their children to wear gendered clothing. After her primary schooling, she and two of her sisters were sent to a higher-education institution that was less focused on higher-education than it was on reforming cultural expectations surrounding gender normativity, hygiene, and education, emboldening Walkers' radical views of femininity. She studied medical literature all her life, and by time she had begun teaching at a local school, she had goals of attending Syracuse Medical College, where she eventually graduated with honors in 1855.

As an adult, Walker continued her refusal of conforming to the standards society expected of her. She often experimented with different lengths of clothes and refused to wear long skirts and other garments because she claimed they limited the mobility of women. She was often criticized by other women for her attire. She was also arrested in New Orleans 1870 for her wardrobe. But despite the hardships, she continued to fight for a reform in women's wear, claiming that clothing should "protect the person, and allow freedom of motion and circulation."

Walker's attire was not the only thing she fought for. During the Civil War, Walker volunteered to be a surgeon for the Army, although she was denied the position because she was a woman. Instead, she was given a civilian nurse position in which she served during the Battle of Bull Run. As she continued to serve, she was promoted to an unpaid field surgeon and eventually to a Contract Acting Assistant Surgeon for the Army of Cumberland, becoming the first woman surgeon to work for the U.S. Army Surgeon. In April of 1864, she was captured as a spy by the Confederate army when she helped a Confederate surgeon conduct an amputation. She was released several months later in a prisoner exchange program. After the war, she continued to fight for dress reform, women's rights, healthcare, and temperance.

A photo of Mary Edwards Walker after her service as a surgeon in the Civil War. After the war, Walker sought a retroactive acknowledgment of her service in the war and was subsequently awarded the Medal of Honor, which can be seen in this photo.

Top: During her service in the Civil War, Walker had the opportunity to meet fellow dress reformist Frances Hook at the Chattanooga war hospital. Hook dressed as a man in order to serve as a Union soldier in the war effort.

Right: Walker was inducted into the National Women's Hall of Fame in 2000. She has many establishments named after her, including the Whitman-Walker Clinic in Washington, D.C., the Army Reserve Center in Walker, Michigan, and the Mary Walker Clinic at the Fort Irwin National Training Center in California.

Heroes of American History 13

Eleanor Roosevelt 1884–1962

Eleanor Roosevelt, born Anna Eleanor Roosevelt, was one of the most influential First Ladies. A niece of Theodore Roosevelt and a distant cousin to Franklin, she grew up in a prominent family, though her parents died when she was young, casting a shadow over her childhood. Her marriage with Franklin had its difficulties, particularly in its early years. Eleanor struggled with an overbearing mother-in-law, finding out that Franklin had had an affair, and his bout with polio. The couple remained together, however, forging a political partnership. Eleanor urged him to remain politically active after the bout with polio. She herself was active in her husband's campaign for governor of New York, and his later campaigns for the presidency.

As First Lady, Roosevelt gave speeches, wrote columns, and advocated for women's and civil rights, becoming a political powerhouse in her own right. At the time, her actions were considered quite controversial. After her husband's death, she remained active, serving as a delegate to the United Nations and later in the Kennedy administration as First Chair of the Presidential Commission on the Status of Women. She died in 1962 at the age of 78.

A photo of fifteen-year-old Eleanor taken while she was a student at London's Allenswood Boarding Academy.

Top: A photo of Eleanor holding a copy of the Universal Declaration of Human Rights, which included Roosevelt's Four Freedoms: 1) the freedom of speech, 2) the freedom of worship, 3) the freedom from want, and 4) the freedom from fear.

Right: A photo of Eleanor and Franklin in 1908 with their first two children.

Ruth Bader Ginsburg 1933–

Ruth Bader Ginsburg was born Joan Ruth Bader in the Flatbush neighborhood of Brooklyn in New York City on March 15, 1933. Her father was a Ukrainian Jewish immigrant and her mother was a first generation Austrian Jew who, although not strictly religious, belonged to the East Midwood Jewish Center where Bader Ginsburg learned the foundations of the Jewish faith and the Hebrew language. She was the second daughter of the Bader family, but her older sister, Marylin, died at the age of six from meningitis. Bader Ginsburg attended James Madison High School, which offered a law program where Bader Ginsburg was introduced to the proceedings of the legal system. After graduating, she enrolled at Cornell University where she would meet her future husband, Martin Ginsburg, join Alpha Epsilon Phi, study government, and graduate as the highest-ranking female of her graduating class.

She and Martin got married one month after graduation in 1954 and had a child one year later while she was working at the Social Security Administration, who demoted Bader Ginsburg while she was pregnant. In 1965, she enrolled in Harvard Law School but then transferred to Columbia Law School in New York and graduated with a Juris Doctor degree, tying for first place in her class. She had initial difficulty finding work after her graduation because of her gender. After years of clerical positions and professorships, Bader Ginsburg co-founded the ACLU's Women's Rights Project in 1973, which worked on hundreds of discrimination cases within the first year of its foundation. Bader Ginsburg herself would win five of the six cases she represented in the Supreme Court between 1973 and 1976. Throughout the 1970s Bader Ginsburg represented multiple cases that touched upon discrimination issues that faced women, advancing the Equal Protection Clause of the Constitution and lessening the difference gap the government placed between men and women.

Bader Ginsburg was diagnosed with colon cancer in 1999, and all throughout her treatment she never missed a day on the job. In 2009, she underwent surgery to remove a tumor in her pancreas. Many believe that she was the first Supreme Court Justice to officiate a same sex marriage in 2013, presiding over the ceremony of Kennedy Center President Michael Kaiser and John Roberts.

In 1980, President Carter elected Bader Ginsburg to the U.S. Court of Appeals for the District of Columbia Circuit, where she often won consensus support over partisan issues. She served on the Court of Appeals until 1993 when she was nominated to the Supreme Court by President Clinton. She is known to be a cautious jurist, but she has continued to weigh in against discrimination on women's issues such as abortion and equal access. She told the *New York Times* in 2009 that "the government has no business making that choice [abortion] for women." In 2018, she came out in support of the #MeToo movement, stating, "It's about time. For so long women were silent, thinking there was nothing you can do about it, but now the law is on the side of women, or men, who encounter harassment, and that's a good thing."

Crazy Horse 1840–1877

Daring and courageous, Crazy Horse rode as a Sioux warrior for more than two decades, counting hundreds of coups. He led his warriors with precise skill against Crow, Shoshone, and white soldiers. In 1866 Crazy Horse and a party of 10 decoys lured Brevet Lieutenant Colonel William J. Fetterman and 80 soldiers into an ambush. Until the Battle of the Little Bighorn, the Fetterman Massacre was the army's worst defeat in the West.

A decade later at the Battle of the Rosebud, Crazy Horse commanded more than 1,200 warriors against General George Crook and his 1,300 soldiers. Crook withdrew after six hours. Eight days later, Crazy Horse provided inspired leadership at the Battle of the Little Bighorn. Despite these victories, the buffalo were virtually exterminated by hide hunters, and in 1877 Crazy Horse was forced to bring his starving people onto the reservation at Fort Robinson, Nebraska.

Soon it was decided by General George Crook to confine the great war leader to the guardhouse. When Crazy Horse went for a knife he was bayoneted fatally, and his parents buried the heart and bones of their 36-year-old son in a secret place.

An alleged photo of Crazy Horse, the Lakota warior and leader.

Top: Frank Leslie's illustration of the Battle of the Rosebud printed in the *Illustrated Newspaper* on August 12, 1876.

Bottom: Brigadier General George Crook served the United States army during the Civil War and the Indian Wars.

Chief Geronimo 1829–1909

The Apache who one day would strike terror into the hearts of Arizona settlers was so placid as a youth that he was called Goyahkla–"One Who Yawns."

At 17 Goyahkla was admitted to the council of warriors. He married, and his wife soon bore him three children. But in 1858 Goyahkla's entire family was slain by Mexican soldiers while the men were absent from their camp in Chihuahua, Mexico.

Stunned by the loss, the One Who Yawns now lusted for vengeance: "My feelings toward the Mexicans did not change–I still hated them and longed for revenge. I never ceased to plan for their punishment." Soon he led a ferocious charge against Mexicans who screamed, "Geronimo!" They were appealing for help to their patron saint, Jerome, or Geronimo in Spanish. Goyahkla's fellow warriors took up the cry, and the One Who Yawns became Geronimo.

Geronimo willingly followed the leadership of Mangas Coloradas and Cochise, and he also led war parties numbering as few as three braves into Mexico. Throughout the 1860s and into the 1870s he looted and killed ceaselessly. Eventually Geronimo took several wives and sired other children, but he could not abandon the warrior's life for long: "I was always glad to fight the Mexicans."

Geronimo was a member of the Bedonkohe band of the Apache tribe and was born in Arizpe, Sonora, in what was then still a territory of Mexico.

Geronimo (right) and his warriors just before they surrendered to General Cook on March 27, 1886, in the Sierra Madre Mountains of Mexico. Geronimo and his troop escaped from captivity three days later. This photo taken by C.S. Fly is one of just a handful of photos that are known to show Native warriors who were still warring against the United States. Most other bands of warriors had surrendered by this time. "We were reckless with our lives, because we felt that every man's hand was against us . . . so we gave no quarter to anyone and asked no favors." --Geronimo

During the 1870s Geronimo moved his family onto a reservation, but occasionally he slipped away on raids, and in 1881 he led a major breakout into Mexico. For more than two years General George Crook led a major military campaign against him. Geronimo finally agreed to meet with Crook, returning to reservation life in 1884, but the next year he again headed for Mexico with another band of diehards. General Nelson Miles and thousands of soldiers pursued Geronimo, along with thousands of Mexicans on the other side of the border. Geronimo submitted to custody in 1886, the last Native American chief to surrender to the army.

Geronimo and his followers were shipped by train to Florida, where he remained for nearly a decade. In 1895 Geronimo was placed on the reservation at Fort Sill, Oklahoma, where he spent the last 14 years of his life. He remained a popular figure at public celebrations, proudly showing off his battle wounds and selling his autograph to fascinated admirers.

Quanah Parker 1845–1911

Quanah ("Sweet Odor") was the son of Comanche chieftain Peta Nocona and Cynthia Ann Parker, who had been abducted by Comanche warriors as a child. Quanah was born about 1845, and later his father and mother produced another son and a daughter.

Quanah grew into a tall, strong man with bold features. He became a splendid rider and was taught to handle the traditional Comanche weapons. By the time Quanah was 15, he had slain his first victim in a raid, and soon he displayed qualities of leadership. During the 1870s Quanah commanded his own war parties and was prominent at the Battle of Adobe Walls in the Texas panhandle in 1874. During the Red River War that followed, a massive military convergence forced Comanche and Kiowa bands onto reservations in southwestern Indian Territory. Quanah and 400 followers were the last to submit, driving 1,500 horses onto the reservation at Fort Sill in May 1875.

Texans referred to their worthy foe as Quanah Parker, emphasizing his white heritage. Still in his 30s, Quanah proved himself a skilled peacetime leader. He sold grazing rights to the 3,000,000-acre reservation lands, extracting lease fees for his people from Charles Goodnight, Burk Burnett, and other cattle barons. These tough businesspeople taught him much about negotiation and subsidized his trips to Washington, D.C., where he sometimes dressed in business suits.

Burnett helped Parker erect the Comanche White House, a rambling 12-room residence near Fort Sill where he installed his vast family (he married 8 times and sired 25 children). Parker's prominence reached celebrity status, and he was in great demand for parades, including President Theodore Roosevelt's 1905 inauguration.

But during all of his interaction with whites, Parker proudly retained much of his Comanche identity, which was a key to his acceptance as tribal leader. He remained polygamous, rejected Christianity, and used peyote and mescal. And when he died of pneumonia in 1911, his demise was presided over by a Comanche medicine man.

Quanah Parker was often criticized by other Comanches for "selling out" to the whites for turning to ranching for an income and wearing suits.

Quanah Parker was elected as the Comanche chief of the reservation by the U.S. government, although Comanches traditionally never followed the rule of one single chief at a time.

Quanah Parker
Chief of the Comanche
Lawton, Okla.

Parker was one of the first prominent leaders in the Native American Church movement, promoting the use of various rituals and beliefs held by many tribes throughout North America. He often said that "the white man goes into his church house and talks about Jesus, but the Indian goes into his tipi and talks to Jesus."

Samuel Gridley Howe 1801–1876

Born in Boston, Massachusetts, on November 10, 1801, Samuel Gridley Howe was the son of a ship-owner and cordage manufacturer. Growing up in the political hotbed of Boston, Howe attended Boston Latin School as an adolescent, and would later enroll at Brown University because his father refused to let his son attend the federalist-influenced Harvard University. He is noted in saying that he regrets not taking his studies more seriously, but he still graduated with a degree in medicine. After graduation, he became enthralled with the Greek Revolution and travelled to Greece to become a wartime surgeon. Although he joined the revolution to contribute his skills as a surgeon, he found that he was needed in more militant roles, leading him to contribute his bravery and enthusiasm to the cause. He travelled back to the U.S. during this period to collect donations in order to help the starving populations of Greece and was able to raise $60,000 for the cause.

After the war he travelled to and from America and Europe, helping raise funds for Polish revolutionaries and establishing two schools for the blind in Paris. After being arrested in Berlin and released due to the intervention of the United States Minister at Paris, Howe retuned to the Boston area and began teaching blind students at his father's house. He soon founded the Perkins Institution, the oldest school for the blind in the U.S., in 1832, which gained momentum quickly and received federal funding the next year. At the school, Howe established the first printing press for the blind in America and used his enthusiasm to make the institution one of the leading centers of philanthropy in the U.S.

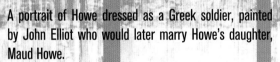

A portrait of Howe dressed as a Greek soldier, painted by John Elliot who would later marry Howe's daughter, Maud Howe.

During the Civil War, Howe worked on the Sanitary Commission which worked to increase sanitary conditions in Union camps to prevent dysentery, typhoid, and malaria.

A photo of the Perkins School for the Blind around 1915 in Watertown, Massachusetts. Today the institution continues to educate the blind and has expanded its resources to online curriculums to help the blind throughout the world.

By the mid-nineteenth century, Howe became a public denouncer of slavery, founding the anti-slavery newspaper *Daily Commonwealth* with his abolitionist wife Julia Ward Howe. He denounced the Fugitive Slave Law, stating "No man's freedom is safe until all men are free." Florence Hall, Howe's daughter, also made claims that the family's home in south Boston was a stop on the Underground Railroad. During the Civil War, Howe served on the American Freedmen's Inquiry Commission where he investigated the lives of Freedmen after slavery in the Deep South and Canada. And after the Civil War he continued the work with the Freedmen's Bureau where he helped emancipated slaves attain education, housing, and employment in the South. Howe remained politically active until his death, advocating for progressive tax systems and serving on President Grant's commission deciding whether or not the U.S. should annex Santo Domingo. He died on January 9, 1876, and is buried at Mount Auburn Cemetery in Cambridge, Massachusetts.

Bayard Rustin 1912–1987

Bayard Rustin was born on March 17, 1912, in West Chester, Pennsylvania, as the ninth of twelve children. Raised by his maternal grandparents, who were wealthy caterers in the West Chester region, Rustin grew up in a household that was very progressive for its day. His grandmother, Julia Rustin, was a practicing Quaker and an active member in the National Association for the Advancement of Colored People (NAACP), who often hosted the likes of W.E.B. Du Bois and James Weldon Johnson in her home. As a youth Rustin spoke out against Jim Crow laws, organized a strike while he was student at the historically black Wilberforce University for the poor quality of food it provided its students, and received activist training from the Quaker run American Friends Service Committee (AFSC), whose goals were to promote peace and social justice in the U.S. and world.

After his training in 1937, Rustin moved to Harlem where he began fighting segregation with various socialist movements, including the Socialist Party of Norman Thomas, a six-time presidential nominee and Presbyterian minister, the Brotherhood of Sleeping Car Porters, and the Fellowship of Reconciliation. Throughout the 1940s, Rustin continued working for social justice in America and impressed the organizer of the Brotherhood of Sleeping Car Porters, A. Philip Randolph, by protecting the property of native-born Japanese Americans who had been sent to internment camps during World War II. Rustin would also be a key organizer in the efforts to desegregate interstate bus travel in what would later be known as the Freedom Rides. Later in the decade he would travel to India to learn of pacifist and non-violent techniques of protest from the Gandhian movement.

Upon returning from India, he contributed to the AFSC's highly circulated pacifist paper, "Speak Truth to Power: A Quaker Search for an Alternative to Violence," in 1955, and was hired to advise Dr. Martin Luther King Jr. in Gandhian pacifism and nonviolence. Together, he and King began organizing the Southern Christian Leadership Conference, but he was forced to resign due to his sexual orientation and political affiliations. But despite the setback, Rustin and his longtime colleague A. Philip Randolph organized the historic March on Washington for Jobs and Freedom in 1963 by coordinating various political, civil rights, labor, and religious movements.

Rustin was not only a civil rights leader in the African American community, but an advocate for the rights of homosexuals in the 1980s. Rustin was often stigmatized for his homosexuality.

Top: After the Civil Rights Act of 1964, Rustin preached that civil rights leaders should strengthen ties with the Democratic party and that nationalistic ideals could be dangerous for excluding possible allies.

Bottom: Rustin organized one of the largest political rallies in American history, the March on Washington for Jobs and Freedom on August 28, 1963. An estimated 250,000 people marched on Washington that day.

Bayard Rustin has largely been forgotten among the seminal figures in the civil rights movement of the mid-twentieth century, but his impact is undeniable. He was a leading force in nonviolent protest methods that propelled civil rights movements toward monumental successes. Rustin died in 1987 of a perforated appendix. His death was announced by President Reagan at the time, and Rustin has received numerous posthumous recognitions.

Heroes of American History 27

Chief Black Kettle 1803–1868

No western chief was more committed to peace with whites than Black Kettle. But he was victimized by two of the most murderous tragedies ever perpetuated upon Native Americans. Chief Black Kettle (also known as Moke-ta-ve-to) perceived the enormous power of whites and determined to avoid conflict for the good of his people. Whenever white soldiers or hunters arrived near his camp in southeastern Colorado, Black Kettle would move his village to avoid any possibility of hostilities. Government officials presented Black Kettle with an enormous U.S. flag, and he proudly flew it from a pole above his tepee.

On two occasions in 1864, Chief Black Kettle used his influence to restrain angry warriors from attacking parties of outnumbered soldiers. But in November 1864, while camped along Sand Creek, his village was attacked by a large force of "Colorado Volunteers" under the command of the vicious Colonel John M. Chivington. With most of the young men absent from camp, Black Kettle's people fled, although more than 150 were killed and mutilated. After dark, he returned to locate his wife. She was still alive, despite being shot nine times. The chief carried her to safety on his back, and miraculously both survived the Sand Creek Massacre. Government commissioners expressed regrets but informed Black Kettle that he must move to a reservation area in American Indian Territory. Other tribes rebelled, but Black Kettle kept his band off the warpath, saying, "Although wrongs have been done me I live in hopes."

But in late 1867 the U.S. Army launched a winter campaign against hostiles, and Lieutenant Colonel George Armstrong Custer led the 7th Cavalry toward Black Kettle's camp on the Washita River. The soldiers struck at dawn on November 27, 1868. Black Kettle fired a warning shot, then leaped onto a horse and pulled his wife up behind him. But he and his wife were shot off their horse, fatally wounded. In all, more than 100 Cheyennes were brutally slain—only 11 of them warriors—and 53 women and children were captured.

Black Kettle was a southern Cheyenne chief who often avoided violence with white settlers in Colorado and sought peace between his people and the U.S. government.

Top: Black Kettle (seated, second from the left) photographed with Cheyenne, Arapaho, and Kiowa chiefs who served on a delegation in Denver, Colorado, to conduct peace talks during the Colorado War of 1864 between Native Americans and white settlers. The agreement established that southern Cheyennes would be relocated to the Sand Creek Reservation.

Bottom: An illustration of the Battle of Washita, where Black Kettle was killed. The battle was initiated by Lt. Colonel Custer's 7th U.S. Calvary, who sought revenge on young bands of Native Americans who continued to raid white settlers despite the peace treaties that had been agreed upon.

THE SEVENTH U.S. CAVALRY CHARGING INTO BLACK KETTLE'S VILLAGE AT DAYLIGHT, November 27, 1868.—[See Page 811.]

Malcolm X 1925–1965

Malcolm X was born Malcolm Little on May 19, 1925, in Omaha, Nebraska. He was the fourth of seven children, and his parents were Baptists and black-activist leaders in their community who raised their children to believe in self-reliance and black pride. Malcolm's family moved quite a bit when he was young because of the threats they received from racist organizations due to his parents' membership to the Universal Negro Improvement Association and their activities within it. They moved from Nebraska to Wisconsin to Michigan and were continually harassed by racist groups after each move. In Lansing, their home was burned down, and Malcolm's father, Earl, blamed the Black Legion, a midwestern white-supremacist group. When Malcolm was six, his father was killed in a streetcar accident, although Malcolm's mother, Louise, believed that his father had been killed by members of the Black Legion. After his father's death, Louise suffered from a nervous breakdown and was committed to the Kalamazoo State Hospital. Malcolm and his siblings were subsequently separated and put in foster homes.

In Malcolm's youth, he faced continuous hardships. He dropped out of school after a teacher of his told him that a black boy shouldn't be studying law. He continued to move around, making it to Boston where he worked various jobs and later to Harlem where he was wrapped up in drug dealing. He soon returned to Boston where he was arrested for burglary and sentenced to eight to ten years. While in prison, Malcolm joined the Nation of Islam, a fledgling religious movement that supported black self-reliance and black-diaspora movements. After joining, he changed his name to Malcolm X, with the X signifying his original African name that would never be known. He was soon put on an FBI watch list after he sent a letter to President Truman vocalizing his opposition to the Korean War and his communist political leanings. Malcolm rose through the ranks of the Nation of Islam and supported its radical teachings that whites were "devils," that blacks were the original people of the world who were superior to whites, and that whites were destined to fall from power.

Malcolm X had enormous effects on the fight for black equality after his death. Many organizations like the Black Power Movement and the Black Arts Movement were inspired by Malcolm X's teachings.

Malcolm X and Martin Luther King Jr. in 1964 before the Senate hearing over the Civil Rights Act. Unlike King, Malcolm X supported a more militant approach to civil rights. He argued that if the American government was unwilling to protect black people, then black people should protect themselves and fight their aggressors, securing freedom "by whatever means necessary."

Malcolm X connected the civil rights movement in America with the global struggle for rights for black people. He was insistent on correcting African Americans who said they were a minority by saying that black people were the majority race on a global scale.

By 1964, Malcolm X became disillusioned with the Nation's teachings and left. He soon met with Martin Luther King Jr.—who Malcolm had previously admonished for his association and collaboration with whites—to discuss civil rights and watch the Senate deliberate the Civil Rights Act. He made a pilgrimage to Mecca and then visited Africa where he met with numerous African leaders. After his visits, he began giving speeches throughout the U.S., advocating for human rights—a term he uses in place of civil rights in order to make the struggle internationally inclusive to all people throughout the world. Tensions between Malcolm X and the Nation of Islam grew and intensified after Malcolm left the organization, and he and his family began to receive death threats from the Nation. On February 21, 1965, Malcolm was shot just before he was to go on stage to speak at the Audubon Ballroom in Manhattan. He was pronounced dead later that day.

Dr. Betty Shabazz 1934–1997

Born in Detroit as Betty Dean Sanders on May 28, 1934, Betty Shabazz spent the first decade of her life with her mother, Ollie Mae Sanders. Ollie Mae abused Betty, and Betty was soon fostered by Lorenzo and Helen Malloy, a wealthy couple who had ties with civil rights groups in the Detroit area. The Malloys kept Betty shielded from the racism that was prevalent in their community and taught her the importance of black self-reliance. It was not until Betty enrolled at the Tuskegee Institute in Alabama that Betty encountered the tensions that existed between whites and blacks in America. Her isolated upbringing did nothing to prepare her for the ferocity of the Southern racism she experienced. The frustration that ensued hindered Betty's studies, and she soon changed her degree from education to nursing. The dean of the nursing school encouraged Betty to transfer to an associated program in Brooklyn, New York.

In 1953, Betty moved to Brooklyn and continued her studies. During her second year at nursing school, a fellow nurse invited Betty to a dinner and lecture organized by the Nation of Islam. It was at one such dinner that Betty met Malcolm X, who was then a minister for the Nation of Islam in New York. Their courtship followed the rules of the Nation of Islam. They enjoyed each other's company in the presence of other members because one-on-one dates were prohibited. They married in 1958 on the same day that Betty received her nursing certificate, and their marriage continued to follow the strict rules of the Nation of Islam, condoning that women should follow the rules laid out by one's husband. But Betty was resilient and soon staked claim for herself in the marriage and made sure Malcolm respected her and met her own expectations of a husband. She and Malcolm worked together for the civil-rights movement and renounced their membership in the Nation of Islam at the same time.

After Malcolm's assassination, Betty raised her daughters, increased her efforts in education, and spoke at a number of engagements in support of civil rights. She later continued her studies, earning a Doctorate in education administration. She began teaching at Medgar Evers College and was soon promoted to the Director of Institutional Advancement and Public Relations, a position she continued to hold until her death. She also volunteered much of her time and served as a committee member of the American Revolution Bicentennial Council and the U.S. Department of Health and Human Services. Betty died in June of 1997 after complications from the burns she received when her house burned down.

Betty Shabazz began teaching at Medgar Evers College in 1976 and served as Director of Institutional Advancement and Public Relations until her death.

Betty Shabazz, Malcolm X, and their family were victims of multiple death threats after they left the Nation of Islam. The family was also surveilled by the FBI at the time.

A photo of Betty Shabazz after she identified the body of her husband, Malcolm X, at the New York City Morgue in February of 1965.

Chief Joseph 1840–1904

The Nez Percé were peaceful Native Americans who inhabited magnificent territory in the Northwest that, in time, became coveted by whites. During negotiations the principled eloquence of a tall young chieftain called Joseph attracted the notice of army officers, government officials, and the nation's press.

The impressive orator was born in 1840 and named Hin-mah-too-yah-latkekt, which meant "Thunder Rolling Down from the Mountains." He was raised in the beautiful Wallowa Mountains, and at the age of 31 succeeded his father, a distinguished leader, as head of the Wallowa band.

Despite Joseph's eloquent diplomacy, the Nez Percé rebelled against white encroachments in 1877. Expertly dueling army contingents along the way as Chief Joseph led their band to Canada, nearly 800 Nez Percé men, women, and children trekked some 1,700 miles before being cut off by General Nelson Miles just 40 miles from Canada. Joseph's brother, the Nez Percé war leader, had been killed, along with the majority of the warriors. Joseph surrendered 431 Nez Percé, including 79 men.

Chief Joseph had not been a combat leader, but abashed army officers portrayed him as a military genius. Through ensuing years Joseph's articulate pleas were ignored and he was never permitted to return to his beloved Wallowa Mountains. But by the time of his death the public had come to regard him as the personification of the noble "red man."

Chief Joseph was chief of the Nez Percé tribe during the tribe's forced removal from their ancestral lands. Joseph led hundreds of tribal members on a retreat to Canada only to be thwarted by the U.S. military.

Top: Chief Joseph and his family around 1880.

Right: Chief Joseph died in exile from his traditional lands from what his doctor called "a broken heart." He has been depicted several times in popular culture, including the film *I Will Fight No More Forever* and the Broadway play *Indians*.

Heroes of American History

Chief John Ross 1790–1866

Born in Turkeytown, Alabama, on October 3, 1790, John Ross was the son of a Cherokee woman and a Scottish immigrant. He was home schooled for much of his life, and he spoke both English and Cherokee. His family household was very much focused around a bicultural upbringing, and when Ross began to attend a schoolhouse, it was a school that taught many bicultural and bilingual students. After he graduated from his school, he served under the command of Andrew Jackson in a Cherokee regiment during the War of 1812. After the war, John Ross showcased his entrepreneurial skills by founding a tobacco farm, trading post, and ferry service along the Tennessee River in 1816. The trading post was located at the mouth of Chattanooga Creek and became a settlement called John's Crossing, known as Chattanooga, Tennessee, today.

Ross served on the Cherokee delegation that began petitioning the U.S. government in Washington, D.C., in 1816. The delegation was formed in order to negotiate border and land ownership issues surrounding the Cherokee tribal territory in the southeastern United States. After he returned from Washington, D.C., he was elected to the National Council of the Cherokee Nation, where he ascended to the council's presidency the following year. Although he was of mixed race, many tribal leaders recognized Ross's skills as a negotiator and his wherewithal to defend the nation against encroaching American policies. John Ross spent the next several years negotiating for the Cherokee Nation with the U.S. government, where he rejected a $200,000 Cherokee relocation buyout and petitioned for the U.S. government to redress the grievances they inflicted upon his people.

Chief John Ross was interred at Ross Cemetery in Indian County, Oklahoma.

Chief John Ross was chosen to be chief of the Cherokee nation in 1828 because of his skills as a negotiator and diplomat.

Many of the early presidents of the U.S. respected the rights Native Americans had to their homelands, but President Andrew Jackson sought to change that policy with the Indian Removal Act of 1830.

John Ross was elected chief of the Cherokee Nation in 1828, and political tensions within the nation soon arose after his election. Chief John Ross continued to face increasing pressure from the U.S. government to relocate the Cherokee people west of the Mississippi River, but with the majority support from council leaders and tribe members, Ross refused. A smaller fraction of leaders, who identified themselves as the Treaty Party, saw the relocation as imminent and supported the negotiations looking for the best deal. Ross's stubborn National Party continued to deny requests for relocation by the U.S. government, but their struggle was lost when members of the Treaty Party signed the Treaty of New Echota and agreed to relocation. Although the treaty was not approved by Chief John Ross or the National Council, the American government saw the treaty as valid. Cherokees were forced to move to Indian Territory in present day Oklahoma by 1838. The Cherokees who remained on their traditional lands after 1838 were forced to relocate by the U.S. army in an event that is now known as the Trail of Tears. After the end of the Civil War, Chief John Ross resumed his position and began travelling to Washington, D.C., again in order to negotiate treaties regarding the Cherokee people. He died during negotiations on August 1, 1866.

Thurgood Marshall 1908–1993

Thurgood Marshall was born in Baltimore, Maryland, on July 2, 1908. His father, William Canfield Marshall, worked for the railroads, while his mother, Norma Arica, was a teacher. Thurgood was introduced to the rhetorical devices of debate at an early age. William would take Thurgood and his brother to watch court proceedings at the local courthouse, and they would then debate the issues later at the dinner table. Both William and Norma instilled such a respect for the United States Constitution and the rule of law in Thurgood at a young age, that he knew full well that he wanted to become a lawyer by the time he applied to the historically-black Lincoln University in Oxford, Pennsylvania. After graduating from Lincoln University with a Bachelor of Arts in Humanities, he then enrolled at the nation's oldest historically-black law program at Howard University in Washington, D.C.

After graduating from Howard, he moved back to Baltimore and began his own law practice. As a young lawyer, he represented the National Association for the Advancement of Colored People (NAACP) in *Murray v. Pearson*, a case that fought to desegregate the law school of the University of Maryland. Marshall won the case, arguing that the "separate but equal" precedent set by *Plessy v. Ferguson* could not be met because the state of Maryland did not provide an equal-in-quality law school for black students. He then quickly ascended from legal staff of the NAACP to Chief Counsel of the NAACP where he argued and won several civil rights cases through the 1940s and 50s, including the monumental *Brown v. Board of Education of Topeka*, which made the continued segregation of public schools in the U.S. illegal.

After 25 years of representing the NAACP, Marshall was appointed to the United States Court of Appeals by President Kennedy in 1961. He was then appointed to the U.S. Solicitor General by President Johnson four years later. And in 1967, he was again appointed by President Johnson to fill the vacant Supreme Court seat after the retirement of Justice Tom C. Clark. As a justice of the Supreme Court, Marshall consistently ruled in support of civil and individual rights. He defended the rights of criminal suspects and opposed the death penalty in almost all circumstances. He served on the court for 24 years until he retired from poor health in 1991. He died from heart failure in 1993 in Bethesda, Maryland, and is buried at Arlington National Cemetery.

When Thurgood Marshall was appointed to the position of U.S. Solicitor General, he was then the highest ranking African-American government official in the U.S. He was also the first African American to be hold a seat on the Supreme Court.

Top: Thurgood Marshall described his judicial philosophy as, "You do what you think is right and let the law catch up." Some conservative opponents have accused Marshall of judicial activism, using his opinion to inform his rulings rather than law. Marshall served on the Supreme Court for 24 years with a liberal record upholding individual rights.

Right: Marshall was married twice in his lifetime and had two sons who have both pursued careers in the U.S. government.

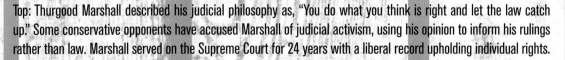

Chief Ouray 1833–1880

Born in 1833 near Taos Pueblo, New Mexico, then known as Nuevo Mexico of the Viceroyalty of New Spain, Ouray grew up in a culturally diverse setting where he learned to speak Ute and Apache languages, sign language, Spanish, and English. His mother died when he was young, and his father moved to become a leader of the Tabeguache Ute band in Colorado, leaving Ouray and his brother to be raised by a Spanish family who owned a ranch near Taos, New Mexico. Ouray received a Catholic education and worked jobs with Mexican sheepherders and pack-mule companies that transported goods on the Santa Fe Trail. By the time Ouray was seventeen, he and his brother went to live with their father's band of Utes, but their father died shortly after their arrival.

Ouray soon rose in the ranks of the Tabeguache, being the band's best horse rider, hunter, and fighter. Ouray was elected to be chief of the band when he was 27. One of his first initiatives as chief was to ease the worries of his tribe members and learn exactly how many whites had settled in the area. He thought that fighting white settlers would not stop the continued settlement and that negotiating with them would be a better way of protecting his tribe's interests. Chief Ouray was a great negotiator due to his even-tempered diplomacy and skills as a polyglot, but many militant Utes thought that he was a coward and tried several times to relieve Ouray of his authority by killing him.

Chief Ouray continually tried to ease the hostilities between members of his Ute tribe and white settlers. He worked with the famous explorer Kit Carson to secure treaties with the U.S. government.

A photo of Ouray (seated, second from the right) and his wife Chipeta (seated, far right) on their last delegation trip to Washington, D.C., in 1880. During this trip, President Hayes described Chief Ouray as the most intellectual man he had ever conversed with.

After his death in 1880, Chief Ouray was buried in a secret location by members of the Ute tribe. In 1925, an official burial ceremony was led by the then leader of the Southern Ute tribe, Buckskin Charley, and Chief Ouray's body was reinterred at Ignacio Cemetery.

Throughout his life, Chief Ouray negotiated many deals with white settlers, forming a strong relationship with Indian Agent, explorer, and icon Kit Carson. With Kit Carson, Chief Ouray drafted treaties that would keep prospectors from mining on the Ute's traditional hunting grounds. Ouray and a delegation of Utes then traveled to Washington, D.C., to present the Treaty of Conejos to President Lincoln in 1863. The treaty lost some of the land that belonged to the Utes, but it secured that their land would not be outright taken from them. Tensions rose in Ute territory as settlers continued to arrive in the area. Ute tribal members contributed to the tribe's troubles by stealing livestock and skirmishing with whites. Chief Ouray continued to negotiate for his tribe diplomatically although the U.S. government continued to approach him asking him to cede more and more Ute land. In 1880, Chief Ouray again traveled to Washington, D.C., and secured three reservations for the Utes in Utah and Colorado. He died from Bright's disease after he returned from the trip.

Jane Addams 1860–1935

Jane Addams was born in Cedarville, Illinois, on September 6, 1860. Her father was a businessman and Illinois State Senator, and was personal friends with Abraham Lincoln. As a child, Addams suffered from tuberculosis that left her with a curved spine, which made it difficult for her to play with other children. She would have lifelong health problems as a result. As a teenager, she read Charles Dickens, and his books inspired a desire to work among the poor. She studied at Rockford Female Seminary, graduating in 1881. That same year her father died, and she inherited $50,000 (about $1.2 million today). Addams attended medical school in Philadelphia, but illness prevented her from completing her degree. In 1887, she travelled with her close friend Ellen Gates Starr to London, where she visited Toynbee Hall. Toynbee was a settlement house; these establishments brought middle-class volunteers to live and work among the poor, providing day care, education, and healthcare. Addams and Starr resolved to start a settlement house in Chicago.

In 1889, Addams and Starr opened Hull House on Chicago's near west side. It was one of the first settlement houses in North America. The settlement was named for the building's original owner, and Addams and Starr organized it to provide services to immigrants and poor residents of the surrounding tenements. The organization eventually grew to more than ten buildings. Hull House provided child care, a public kitchen, educational classes, an art gallery, a summer camp, and social programs. Hull House built the first public playground in the city, and established a theater group that has been credited as the founder of the American "Little Theatre" movement.

At the outbreak of World War I, Addams became the chair of the Women's Peace Party, and spoke regularly on pacifism. In 1915, she attended the International Congress of Women at the Hague with social reformers Emily Greene Balch and Alice Hamilton.

Top: From 1919 to 1929, Addams was president of the International Committee of Women for a Permanent Peace. She shared the Nobel Peace Prize in 1931 for her work promoting pacifism.

Right: Addams served on the Chicago Board of Education beginning in 1905, chairing the Board's School Management Committee. In 1910, she was elected the first female president of the National Conference of Social Work, and the next year she established the National Federation of Settlements, which she led for more than twenty years.

Addams and Starr also provided emergency medical services when doctors were not available, often volunteering as midwives and nurses. Hull House also was one of the first organizations that sheltered victims of domestic violence. Hull House advocated for the people it served, leading efforts to pass legislation at all levels of government on child welfare, women's suffrage and healthcare and immigration reform. Many of the Hull House buildings were torn down when the University of Illinois at Chicago was built in 1963. The original Hull House remains on Halsted Avenue on the near west side, and is now a museum. Jane Addams died on May 21, 1935, in Chicago, Illinois.

Harriet Tubman 1822–1913

In 1849, Tubman herself was a slave. She escaped her plantation existence in Maryland by stealing away into the surrounding forests, ultimately making her way to the free state of Pennsylvania. When the Civil War began in 1861, the 40-year-old Tubman was already the most famous black woman in America. Tubman's burning desire to assist her family and other slaves in the South was her motivation during the 12 years she led slaves to freedom—she did not work for reward or commercial gain. Tubman kept virtually no records of her secret missions to the South, and there is no precise accounting of the number of slaves she assisted to freedom. Some evidence suggests that Tubman made at least 20 different trips down south.

Tubman's fame and success in infiltrating Southern slave holdings during the early 1850s caused blacks to revere her and the plantation aristocracy to hate her. One Maryland slave owner offered a reward of $40,000—about $1 million by today's standards—for her capture. This development prompted Tubman, somewhat wisely, to move to the small Canadian city of St. Catherines, just across Niagara Falls from Buffalo, New York, which was a popular northern terminus for the Underground Railroad. She lived there from 1851 to 1857. After working as an army nurse, Tubman was asked in 1862 to conduct a number of scouting and spying missions in the Southern states. Her experiences with the Underground Railroad were great training for this military spy and reconnaissance work.

Although Tubman was offering freedom to her Underground Railroad passengers, she was ruthless with her human cargo. If escaping slaves seemed overly fearful or were inclined to return to their owner, Tubman would brandish a loaded revolver to change their minds. She was proud that every slave she assisted was delivered to freedom.

Tubman (seen on the left) with her family. Her husband, Davis, is the man seated closest to her.

In 1851, abolitionist John Brown declared that "slavery is war," and Tubman likely believed the same thing. She conducted her raids like a guerilla fighter, often in disguise, using the fields and forests as her cover.

Official Union records list Tubman as an "advisor" to Colonel James Montgomery in a combined gunboat and land mission against Confederate positions near South Carolina's Combahee River on June 2, 1863. In fact, the mission was the first American military engagement of any significance to be planned and directed by a woman.

Harriet Tubman's contributions to both the freedom of slaves and the Union war effort were profound. After the war, she remained busy. During Reconstruction, she established schools to educate former slaves. She also helped found an old age home in Auburn, New York. Despite her achievements, however, Tubman received little public acclaim and lived a long life of relative poverty. Her memoir, *Scenes in the Life of Harriet Tubman*, only attracted much attention after she died in 1913 at age 93.

Heroes of American History   45

Red Cloud 1822–1909

Red Cloud spent the first half of his long life as a free Oglala Sioux, a gifted warrior and hunter who reveled in the exhilarating life of the horse Indians of the northern Plains. He claimed his first scalp when he was 16. During a raid against the Crows he boldly killed the enemy chief, and on another raid he killed four Pawnee braves. By the 1860s Red Cloud was battling white soldiers. Widely acknowledged as the best war leader of the Oglala, he soon commenced a bloody and successful campaign known as Red Cloud's War.

In the early 1860s the Bozeman Trail to Montana's gold fields cut through some of the richest hunting grounds of the Sioux and Cheyenne. Red Cloud and other leaders harassed travelers on the trail, and in 1865 the U.S. government began erecting a series of protective forts. Red Cloud extended his guerrilla war from white travelers to the soldiers. In 1866 the warriors annihilated an 80-person column from Fort Phil Kearny, and Red Cloud continued to send his warriors against civilians and soldiers at every opportunity. Finally the War Department relented. In 1868 the Bozeman Trail forts were abandoned, and the trail was closed. Red Cloud had engineered the only successful campaign waged by Native Americans against the U.S. Army.

But Red Cloud's triumph proved hollow as the Sioux culture was threatened by the unending encroachment of whites and the accelerating disappearance of the buffalo herds. In 1870 Red Cloud traveled by train to Washington, D.C., to appeal to another great warrior, President Ulysses S. Grant. This trip, and six other visits to the capital, made him realize the extent of his enemy's size and power. Although he stated his intention to fight to the death rather than submit, his responsibilities as a leader impelled him to bring his people onto reservations. For the last four decades of his life, Red Cloud was subjected to maddening injustice from whites and to endless criticism from discontented Sioux. His death in 1909 probably brought welcome relief to the old chief.

Red Cloud was a leader of the Oglala Lakota who fought in several battles against the U.S. military before becoming a diplomat for his tribe during the establishment of the Great Sioux Reservation in 1868.

Top: Chief Red Cloud was baptized as a Catholic, but he continually fought for his tribe's rights to their land.

Left: Red Cloud, on the right, with American Horse, an Oglala Lakota chief, historian, and educator who promoted friendly cooperation with settlers.

Heroes of American History 47

Sitting Bull 1831–1890

Sitting Bull was born in what is now South Dakota in 1831. His father, Returns Again, was a Hunkpapa Lakota warrior of high regard. In his early twenties, he became the leader of the Lakota Strong Heart Society, the warrior class of the tribe. During the Dakota War of 1862–1864, Sitting Bull encountered American soldiers for the first time, leading the defense of a small village against an attack by 4,000 U.S. troops in the Battle of Killdeer Mountain.

In the 1870s, gold was discovered in the Black Hills. Prospectors poured into the area, and the U.S. government abandoned the treaty and declared war on any Natives who resisted attempts to seize the land. During the fall of 1875, Natives from Lakota and other tribes arrived at Sitting Bull's camp. In June 1876 they held a ritual Sun Dance at the camp to prepare to defend their land. At the gathering, Sitting Bull danced for three days, during which time he had a vision in which the warriors defeated the Army.

Several days after the Sun Dance, a force led by General George Crook was attacked by Lakota warriors at Rosebud creek, forcing the Army to retreat after a long and bloody battle. A week later, General George Armstrong Custer encountered Sitting Bull's camp near the mouth of the Little Bighorn River. Not realizing the size of the force, Custer attacked. Sitting Bull led thousands of Lakota and Cheyenne warriors in a devastating counterattack that annihilated Custer's forces in an overwhelming victory. Custer was killed along with more than 250 of his men.

Initially, Sitting Bull was called "Slow" because he did not show much talent for battle. When he was ten years old, he killed his first buffalo, and at fourteen he fought well in a battle against a rival tribe. Following the battle he was renamed Tatanka Iyotanka, or "Buffalo Who Sits Down."

"SITTING BULL"
(Ta-Ton-ka-I-yo-ton-ka,)
The Sioux Chief in command at the Custer Massacre.
ZIMMERMAN BROS., Publishers.   Photographed by O. S. GOFF.
Copyright applied for.

The United States responded to the defeat by flooding the Black Hills with troops, forcing many of the Lakota to surrender. In 1877, Sitting Bull led his band into Canada, where he remained for the next four years. In 1881 he returned to the Dakota Territory and was imprisoned for two years. In 1885 he joined Buffalo Bill's Wild West Show, but he soon grew disillusioned with the performance and returned to the Lakota land, where he lived in a cabin on the Grand River.

In 1889, the government grew fearful that Sitting Bull would join the burgeoning Ghost Dance movement, a spiritual movement that preached a return of Native lands to the Lakota. They sent police to arrest Sitting Bull on December 15, 1890. When Sitting Bull resisted, the police shot him in the head and chest, killing him.

Left: Sitting Bull and his family 1881 at Fort Randall.

Right: In 1884 Sitting Bull was hired by promoter Alvaren Allen to tour the U.S. and Canada in his own version of a wild west show called the Sitting Bull Connection. In 1885, he joined Buffalo Bill Cody's Buffalo Bill's Wild West.

Heroes of American History

Helen Keller 1880–1968

Helen Keller was born on June 27, 1880, in Tuscumbia, Alabama, to Arthur Keller, a newspaper editor and former captain of the Confederate Army, and Catherine Everett Keller, daughter of the Confederate General Charles W. Adams. At 19 months of age, it is suspected that Helen contracted either meningitis or scarlet fever, which left her deaf and blind. By 1886, Helen had several dozen signs she could use to communicate with her family, and her mother soon began seeking recommendations on how to educate Helen. Travelling to Baltimore to see specialists, the family was referred to Alexander Graham Bell, who was teaching deaf children at the time, who then referred the family to the Perkins Institute for the Blind. The director of the Perkins Institute for the Blind assigned a former student of the institute, Anne Sullivan, who was visually impaired, the task of educating Helen.

Anne moved into the Keller home and began teaching Helen by spelling words into the palm of Helen's hands. Keller was initially frustrated because she did not understand that every object had a corresponding word to identify it, but after several breakthroughs, Helen quickly began learning the words of the objects in her everyday life. Helen and Anne then moved to Boston so Helen could attend the Perkins Institute, and then they moved to New York in 1894 for Helen to attend the Wright-Humason School for the Deaf. Just a few years later, Helen was admitted to Radcliffe College, Harvard University's liberal-arts college for women, where she would graduate four years later with a Bachelor of Arts degree, making her the first deaf-blind person in the nation to receive the degree.

After graduation, Helen learned to speak and began lecturing about her life. She became a prominent social activist and author who fought for the rights of people with disabilities and women. Her writings often spoke out against military intervention and warfare. She co-founded Helen Keller International, which researches nutrition and the difficulties of blindness, and the American Civil Liberties Union. She was a member of the Socialist party and held many radical views for her time that supported pacifism, birth control, and women's suffrage. She was awarded the Presidential Medal of Freedom by President Johnson and was elected into the National Women's Hall of Fame in 1965. After suffering from several strokes in 1961, she lived the rest of her life at her home until she died in her sleep in 1968.

Helen Keller as a young girl in 1888 with her teacher Anne Sullivan.

Top: Hellen Keller was a political activist in the late nineteenth and early twentieth centuries who spoke out in favor of pacifism, the suffragette movement, worker's rights, women's rights, and socialism. She was the first deaf-blind person to receive a Bachelor of Arts degree.

Left: Helen Keller had friendships with other radicals and revolutionaries of her time, including Mark Twain and Alexander Graham Bell. Mark Twain introduced Keller to Henry Rogers, an oil magnate who would pay for her college education at Radcliffe College.

Aldo Leopold 1887–1948

Rand Aldo Leopold, born in 1887, grew up in Iowa and—ironically perhaps—was a hunter. With an aim to ensure that wildlife remained wild (and likewise, fruitful for hunters), Leopold joined the U.S. Forest Service shortly after graduating from Yale. His first assignment? Managing the Arizona territories, including its timber and what he then called "varmints"—wolves, coyotes, and other predatory animals that preyed on valuable livestock and game. His attitude was in line with the common thinking of the time: Wildlife had to be controlled in order to protect the interests of man.

It's possible that a long bout of nephritis—which struck Leopold after being caught in a flood and blizzard in 1913—gave him time to reflect. Perhaps the crisis of World War I broadened his view. Whatever the impetus, Leopold, who had married and become a father, recovered his health, resumed his work with the Forest Service, and began to see conservation as more than a matter of economics. It was in Wisconsin that the seeds of Leopold's brave new thinking took root and blossomed. As a professor of game management at the University of Wisconsin-Madison, Leopold penned the revolutionary book *Game Management* which was published in 1933. Part philosophy and part how-to manual of skill and technique, Leopold's book began shaping the conservation ethic—the notion that humans and wilderness exist in a state of mutual interdependence and that it is a privilege, not an obligation, to bend the earth to people's will.

In 1935, he purchased a small square of worn-out former farmland alongside the Wisconsin River near Baraboo. On the grounds were the remains of a dilapidated old chicken coop, where Leopold, his wife, Estella, and their five children would stay during their visits. Though the family fixed it up, the coop's nickname—"The Shack"—remained. The family retreated to the land on weekends and school vacations to relax, explore, and, in typical Leopold fashion, to experiment.

Aldo Leopold and his wife Estella Bergere. They married in 1912 in New Mexico where Leopold worked at the Carson National Forest.

Leopold in the Sierra Madre Mountains of Mexico in 1936.

Aldo Leopold and his family in front of "The Shack" on their land near Baraboo, Wisconsin. All of Aldo and Estella's children became educators and naturalists.

Leopold saw the exhausted land as an outdoor laboratory, a living workshop in which he could test his ideas about restoring health to the depleted earth. He and his family enriched the soil, built a garden, cut firewood, fought drought, and planted prairie grasses, flowers, hardwoods, and conifers—nearly 40,000 pines alone. This life-size, and lifelong, test of Leopold's land proved fruitful. He eventually transformed the farm into a healthy, thriving landscape and in the process helped shape many of the environmental restoration techniques used today. Sadly, Leopold didn't live to see all that his little plot of land on the Wisconsin River would come to mean to the world; he died of a heart attack while struggling to fight a brush fire that was encroaching on his land in 1948.

Ida B. Wells 1862–1931

Our culture's pantheon of fame may only have room for a limited number of individuals, but Ida B. Wells should certainly be included among this honorable group. She was born in 1862 to slave parents who were freed along with the rest of America's slaves in 1865. When Wells was 16, her parents and youngest sibling died during a yellow fever epidemic. In order to keep her family together, Wells showed her budding strength as she took a job as a schoolteacher and raised her younger siblings.

Wells moved her family to Memphis, Tennessee; it was here that she experienced the act of racism that launched her career. Wells had bought a first-class train ticket for a "ladies'" car, but the conductor told her to move to the "colored" car to make room for a white man. When Wells refused, the conductor attempted to forcibly move her. As Wells explained in her autobiography, "the moment he caught hold of my arm I fastened my teeth in the back of his hand." It took two more men to drag her off the conductor and off the train.

Wells sued the railroad company; she won the case in lower courts but lost the case when it was appealed to the Supreme Court of Tennessee. But the case served to instigate the fight for equality. Wells became the co-owner and editor of *Free Speech*, an anti-segregationist newspaper in Memphis. She focused her energies on revealing the widespread horrors of lynching.

Wells was the first scholar of note to unearth the hypocrisy behind the white man's so-called protection of white women's honor through lynching: "To justify their own barbarism," Wells wrote, "they assume a chivalry they do not possess...no one who reads the record, as it is written in the faces of the million mulattoes in the South, will for a minute conceive that the southern white man had a very chivalrous regard for the honor due the women of his own race, or respect for the womanhood which circumstances placed in his power." Wells concluded that the brutal lynching epidemic was really the result of fear for economic competition, combined with white men's anger at voluntary liaisons between white women and black men and a large helping of racism.

SOUTHERN HORRORS.

LYNCH LAW

IN ALL

ITS PHASES

MISS IDA B. WELLS,

The cover of *Southern Horrors: Lynch Laws in All Its Phases*, where Wells argued that white populations accused black men of raping white women to hinder the economic progress of the black population.

Top: Ida B. Wells was a founding member of the NAACP, along with W.E.B. Du Bois, Archibald Grimke, Mary Church Terrell.

Right: Ida B. Wells and her four children in Chicago in 1909. During Chicago's World's Columbian Exposition in 1893, Wells and other black leaders boycotted the fair for its exclusion of African Americans from its exhibits.

Wells' work for civil rights continued until her death in 1931. She married fellow activist and writer F. L. Barnett in 1895. Together the couple had four children and worked to help the African-American community in Chicago. Wells also was a founding member of the NAACP and the first president of the Negro Fellowship League. In 1930, shortly before her death, she ran for the Illinois Senate. Wells's resume is extensive and her activism was effective, and she certainly earned her right to the hall of fame of civil rights leaders.

Heroes of American History   55

John Muir 1838–1914

John Muir was born in Scotland on April 21, 1838. When he was eleven, his family immigrated to the United States, settling in Wisconsin. Muir worked on his family farm until he attended the University of Wisconsin at 22. In 1867, while he was working in a wagon-wheel factory, he was injured and nearly lost his sight. Upon recovering, he determined to follow his dream of wandering the natural spaces of the nation.

Upon seeing Yosemite for the first time in 1868, he was overwhelmed by its pristine valley and soaring mountain peaks. Muir built a small cabin along Yosemite Creek, and lived there for the next two years. During this time, he explored Yosemite's high country, often alone, carrying nothing but a loaf of bread, a handful of tea, a tin cup, and a copy of Ralph Waldo Emerson's writings. He'd often spend the night sitting in his overcoat next to a campfire, reading Emerson. He was often visited by scientists, naturalists, and artists. In 1871, he was visited by Emerson himself.

In order to protect his beloved Yosemite and promote preservation of natural spaces, Muir co-founded the Sierra Club in 1892. The organization fought to protect the Park from grazing and prevent it from being reduced in size. In 1889, a series of Muir's articles appeared in *Century* magazine that highlighted the devastation of the meadows and forests of Yosemite by sheep and cattle grazing. Working with *Century*'s editor Robert Underwood Johnson, Muir was able to convince Congress to create Yosemite National Park. Muir would eventually be involved in the creation of the Sequoia, Petrified Forest, Grand Canyon, and Mount Rainer National Parks as well.

In 1901, he published *Our National Parks*, which prompted President Theodore Roosevelt to visit him in Yosemite. Upon entering the park, Roosevelt asked Muir to show him "the real Yosemite," and the two set off alone to hike through the back country. They talked late into the night, and slept under the stars at Glacier Point. The experience, and Muir's advocacy, convinced Roosevelt to create the National Parks Service and put Yosemite and other Parks under Federal protection. Muir died in Los Angeles on Christmas Eve, 1914.

After his first visit to Yosemite, Muir built a cabin along Yosemite Creek where he lived for two years. The cabin was simple, but Muir built it in such a way that the creek flowed through one corner of the house so that he could listen to the water running. Muir's time in this cabin is captured in his book *First Summer in Sierra*.

John Muir once undertook a thousand-mile walk from Indianapolis to Florida. He then sailed to Cuba, and then to New York, where he booked passage to San Francisco. It was in California that he would find his true home in the Sierra Nevada and Yosemite.

John Muir accompanied President Roosevelt to the Yosemite region in 1903. They met in Oakland, California, booked passage to Raymond by rail, and then travelled by stagecoach to the future national park. During their travels, Muir talked to Roosevelt about the state's mismanagement of the land and the exploitation of the valley's resources.

Heroes of American History   57

Marjory Stoneman Douglas 1890–1998

Marjory Stoneman Douglas was born in Minneapolis, Minnesota, on April 7, 1890, to Frank Bryant Stoneman and Florence Lillian Trefethen, a concert violinist. She was the couple's only child and became a rapacious reader at a young age. One of her earliest memories was of picking an orange from a tree in Tampa, Florida, the state that she would later center her career as an environmental activist around. In 1908 she attended Wellesley College, an all-woman liberal-arts college in Massachusetts, where she attained straight *As* and graduated with a Bachelor of Arts degree in 1912.

By 1915, Stoneman moved to Miami when the town still had fewer than 10,000 residents in it. She began working for the *Miami Herald* as a culture reporter. Instead of writing about everyday events in the then news-lacking city, she wrote about prominent women in the area who held leadership roles. After years of reporting, she began freelance writing and working as an environmental activist to save the Everglades from being destroyed by development. After being approached to contribute to a series of essays about American rivers, she began researching the Miami River and subsequently the Everglades. She viewed the Everglades as an incredibly unique ecological site that was mismanaged and mistreated by local officials. Talk of draining the Everglades had been about for decades, and local politicians continuously sold off sections of it to developers, but Stoneman knew that such actions would be the cultural, economic, and environmental downfall of South Florida.

Marjory Stoneman Douglas's senior portrait at Wellesley College.

In 1947, Stoneman published *The Everglades: River of Grass*, which argued that the Everglades were not only a unique ecological system that should be saved, but also that the destruction of the Everglades would deprive South Florida of its freshwater resources. Much of her subsequent work went to protecting this vital and unique ecological destination. She was a member of Everglades Tropical National Park Committee, and she founded the Friends of the Everglades in 1969 in order to protest the proposed building of a jet port in Big Cypress Swamp. She continually fought against any action that threatened the health of the Everglades, and eventually had to move her initiative from conserving the Everglades to restoring the Everglades due to the damage that was inevitably done to the region. She was awarded the Presidential Medal of Freedom by Bill Clinton when she was 103 years old, and she was posthumously inducted into the National Wildlife Federation's Hall of Fame. She died at the age of 108 on May 14, 1998.

Top: A photo of her parents' extended family in 1893. The three-year-old Marjory is being held by her father on the far right.

Left: A photo of Marjory Stoneman Douglas at a 1985 ceremony in which the Department of Natural Resources named their administrative building after her. The National Parks Conservation Association has also named an award after her which is given to people who protect the National Park System. Marjory Stoneman Douglas High School in Parkland, Florida, was named after her and opened in 1999. Unfortunately the school made news in 2018 after a mass shooting took place there.

Charlotta Bass 1874–1969

Charlotta Bass was born to Hiram and Kate Spears, the sixth of eleven children, in Sumter, South Carolina, on February 14, 1874. She attended public schools in her youth and only attended one semester of college, at Penbroke University, before she began her career in publishing. At the age of 20, she moved to Providence, Rhode Island, and worked alongside her brother at the *Providence Watchman* for ten years. She moved to California for health-related issues and soon got a job selling subscriptions to the *California Eagle*. Charlotta Bass then assumed the position of editor-in-chief of the paper after the paper's owner, John Neimore, died. She bought the paper at auction for $50 in 1912, becoming the first African-American woman in the U.S. to own a newspaper. Along with her husband Joseph Bass, who she hired as an editor in 1912, Charlotta focused the scope of the paper around issues concerning racial discrimination and injustice in the community.

The *California Eagle* gave Charlotta an outlet to criticize issues concerning African Americans, including D.W. Griffith's racist film *The Birth of a Nation*, which inspired the reformation of the Ku Klux Klan. Other issues that she attacked with her paper were discriminatory housing and hiring practices in Los Angeles, discrimination against Asian- and Mexican-American citizens, and segregated practices that were in place in schools and hospitals. Bass became the co-president of the Los Angeles chapter of the Universal Negro Improvement Association, founded the Home Protective Association to eliminate all-white neighborhoods, and co-founded the Industrial Business Council to promote and support black business owners. Because of her activites, Bass was monitored by the FBI as a suspected communist from the 1940s until the end of her life–intelligence agencies even began to believe that the *California Eagle* was funded by Japanese and German propagandists.

Charlotta Bass was a publisher, activist, and politician who fought for and promoted the ideas of civil rights in the mid-twentieth century. She was the first African-American woman to both own a newspaper and run for vice-president of the United States.

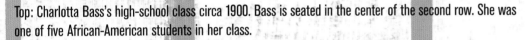
Top: Charlotta Bass's high-school class circa 1900. Bass is seated in the center of the second row. She was one of five African-American students in her class.

Right: A photo of Bass with Paul Robeson, an actor and civil-rights activist, in 1949.

Charlotta became active in politics in the 1940s when she worked as west-coast director of the presidential campaign for Wendell Willkie. She then became a jurist on the Los Angeles County Court system and organized protests at the mayor's office to expand the city's Committee of American Unity to create a stronger dialogue in the community surrounding civil rights. She changed her political affiliation from the Republican party to the Progressive party because she believed that both the Democratic and Republican parties did not do enough to address racial injustices. She became the National Chairman of the Sojourners for Truth and Justice, an all-black group of women that fought racial discrimination, in 1952. That same year she became the first African-American woman to run for vice-president in support of Progressive candidate Vincent Hallinan. During the last years of her life, she maintained a library in her garage for the youth in her neighborhood. She died in 1969 from a cerebral hemorrhage and is buried at Evergreen Cemetery in Los Angeles.

Heroes of American History 61

Maria Mitchell 1818–1889

Maria Mitchell was born on the island of Nantucket, off the coast of Massachusetts, on August 1, 1818 to William and Lydia Mitchell. Brought up in the Quaker religion, which supported the equal education of boys and girls, Mitchell was given a strong education in math and astronomy under the oversight of her father, who was active in the public-education system on the island. She attended the island's North Grammar school, where her father William was principal, until her father opened his own school when Maria was 11 years old. At her father's school, Maria became a teacher's assistant and began using her father's telescope to make astronomical observations.

Maria excelled in astronomical concepts at an early age, helping her father predict the exact time of the next solar eclipse when she was 12 years old. In 1847, when Maria was in her late twenties, Maria discovered comet C/1847 T1, or Miss Mitchell's Comet, using a Dollond refracting telescope. The announcement of her discovery was submitted by her father to *Sillman's Journal*, which would later come to be known as the *American Journal of Science*. Maria then published her calculations of the comet's orbit, confirming that she had indeed discovered a new comet. A celebration of her discovery was held at the Seneca Falls Convention, the famous convention convened to promote women's rights, in July of 1848. Maria gained international fame when she became the recipient of an award established by King Frederick VI of Denmark for new astronomical discoveries.

After her discovery, Mitchell was admitted to the American Academy of the Arts and Sciences in 1848, the American Association of the Advancement of Science in 1850, and the American Philosophical Society in 1869—quite often the first women in the ranks of the associations. She was the first woman to gain a faculty position at Vassar College in 1865, where she and her students began taking the first photographs of the sun to observe sunspots. Mitchell retired from Vassar College in 1888, moved to Lynn, Massachusetts, with her sister's family, and then died of a brain disease in 1889. She is buried at Prospect Hill Cemetery on Nantucket.

After Maria Mitchell won King Frederick VI of Denmark's award for her discovery, American astronomy was legitimized in the eyes of the continental Europeans who had dominated the field for much of the field's history.

The Observatory at Birthplace of Maria Mitchell, Nantucket, Mass.

66799

66799

Top Left: Today, the Maria Mitchell Observatory serves as a public education resource on Nantucket and is built on the site of Maria Mitchell's birthplace.

Top Right: Maria Mitchell is seen here seated at the foot of the telescope at Vassar College with her student Mary Watson Whitney, who would later go on to become the head of Vassar College's Observatory.

Left: Maria Mitchell was the third woman in history to discover a comet, after Caroline Herschel's discoveries in the late eighteenth century and Maria Margarethe Kirch's discoveries in the early eighteenth century.

Albert Einstein 1879–1955

Born in the German Kingdom on March 14, 1879, Albert Einstein held many citizenships, but it would be the United States in which he would spend the last 20 years of his life. Einstein grew up as a non-observant Ashkenazi Jew and attended Catholic schools in his youth. He had an aptitude for mathematics and science and it is said that he found independent proof of the Pythagorean theorem when he was 12. At age 16, he was admitted to the Swiss Federal Polytechnic in Zurich where he excelled in physics and mathematics. That same year, he renounced his German citizenship to avoid military service. After graduating, Einstein sought a teaching post to no avail and began working in a patent office in Bern, Switzerland.

It was during his work in the patent office that Einstein began publishing academic papers concerning physics. In 1905, he defended his thesis paper, "A New Determination of Molecular Dimensions," which resulted in Einstein's attainment of a PhD from the University of Zurich. Later that same year, he published the *Annus Mirabilis* papers which included Einstein's most famous work, including the theory of special relativity and the matter-energy equivalence (or famously known by the legant equation of $E = mc^2$). By 1908, Einstein was recognized throughout the academic world and received a teaching position in physics at the University of Bern. A year later he was promoted to the new faculty position within the field of theoretical physics. By 1921, Einstein had won the Nobel Prize for his discoveries documented in the *Annus Mirabilis*.

Einstein was a pivotal figure in the development of quantum physics with his discoveries of general relativity, special relativity, the photoelectric effect. Throughout his life he sought to close the gaps between Newtonian mechanics and the electromagnetic field.

Top: Einstein's books were often subject to the book burnings held in Nazi Germany. It was Hitler's rise to power in Germany which forced Einstein to become an American citizenship and leave his life in Europe behind. Here we see Einstein being granted his U.S. citizenship by Judge Phillip Forman in 1940.

Left: Einstein was a pacifist and saw war as a disease that must be resisted. He appreciated the meritocracy of the U.S. that promoted the nation's innovative character. He was a member of the National Association for the Advancement of Colored People and worked for civil rights in the nation alongside W.E.B. Du Bois.

Einstein lectured to the greatest scientific communities around the world, and in 1933, as Hitler took power in Germany, Einstein found himself in America, unwilling to return to Europe due to the threat that now faced him as a person of Jewish heritage. He took a job at the Institute for Advanced Study in Princeton, New Jersey, where he continued to work until his death. During World War II, Einstein was informed of the implications his work had on the development of atomic weapons. As a pacifist, Einstein agreed to write a letter, along with Leo Szilard, warning the U.S. government about the dangers of losing the atomic race to Germany. The letter was delivered to President Roosevelt, who soon initiated the Manhattan Project. Einstein saw this as one the gravest mistakes of his life. By addressing the threat of an atomic-armed Germany, he promoted the eventual development of the world's most deadly weapon. Einstein would eventually see the deployment of America's atomic bombs over Japan at the end of World War II, regretting the fruit that his genius bore. Einstein died in 1955 from an aneurysm, and his ashes were spread at an undisclosed location.

George Washington Carver 1864–1943

George Washington Carver was born in Diamond, Missouri, on an unknown date sometime before the end of slavery in 1865. He was born into slavery on the estate of Moses Carver, who had bought George's parents, Mary and Giles, in 1855 for $700. After the end of slavery, George was raised by Moses Carver and his wife, who continued to influence George and encourage him to pursue education. He studied at various segregated schools in the region, moved in with another foster family in Fort Scott, Kansas, and eventually graduated with a high-school degree from Minneapolis High School in Minneapolis, Kansas. He applied for many colleges as a young man, and was admitted to Highland University in Kansas before his admittance was rescinded when they learned he was African American.

In 1886, Carver homesteaded a claim in Kansas where he created a conservatory of plants and farmed Native American corn, rice, and other produce. He then received a loan to educate himself and attended Simpson College in Iowa to study art and piano before he was encouraged to study botany by a professor who noticed Carver's knack for painting flowers and plants. He transferred to Iowa State University, then the Iowa State Agriculture College, where he received a Master's Degree in science and became the school's first African-American faculty member. In 1896, Carver was invited by Booker T. Washington, the then president of the Tuskegee Institute, to become the head of the school's Agriculture Department. There he taught about crop rotation, alternatives to cash crops, soil restoration, and self-sufficiency to his students and local farmers for 47 years.

George Washington Carver was admitted to the Royal Society of the Arts in 1916, one of only a handful of American members at the time. His gained renown throughout the world's scientific communities because of his work with peanuts that led to a better understanding of ecology and sustainable agriculture.

Top: George Washington Carver seen seated in the center of the front row with his fellow faculty members at the Tuskegee Institute in Alabama in 1902.

Bottom: A pamphlet from 1943 featuring George Washington Carver, "one of America's great scientists."

DR. CARVER HAS CREATED SOME 200 PRODUCTS FROM THE LOWLY PEANUT, AND OVER 100 FROM THE SWEET POTATO.

HERE ARE A FEW OF THEM:

MILK
BUTTER
CHEESE
COFFEE
PICKLES
FLOUR
SOAP
INK
COSMETICS
SHAVING LOTION
BREAKFAST FOOD
STARCH
VINEGAR
SHOE-BLACKING
LIBRARY PASTE
CANDY

MANY OF HIS PRODUCTS ARE NOW AIDING THE WAR EFFORT.

Who Knows ??

HE MAY YET GIVE UNCLE SAM THE RUBBER HE SO URGENTLY NEEDS!!

KIDNAPPED AS A BABY BY NIGHT RAIDERS, HE WAS RANSOMED BY HIS OWNER, MOSES CARVER, FOR A RACE HORSE, VALUED AT $300.

George Washington Carver

One of America's Great Scientists

HE NOT ONLY TAUGHT SOUTHERN FARMERS SOIL CONSERVATION—HE GAVE THE SOUTH A NEW AND LUCRATIVE INDUSTRY—PEANUT PRODUCTS, YIELDING OVER $60,000,000 ANNUALLY.

A majority of Carver's influence came from his work in restoring soil quality after multiple cotton yields deprived the soil of nutrients. Carver promoted the planting of peanuts, soy beans, and sweet potatoes to restore the soil's nitrogen levels and improve its agricultural health. He founded industrial research facilities to find new products that can be made from these alternative crops, printed pamphlets of recipes to improve the health of Southern African Americans, and formed an extension program at the Tuskegee Institute to teach local farmers how to rotate their crops. Carver died on January 5, 1943, after falling down a flight of stairs at home. He is buried next to Booker T. Washington at the Tuskegee Institute.

Lewis Howard Latimer 1848–1928

Lewis Howard Latimer was born on September 4, 1848, in Chelsea, Massachusetts. He was the youngest of Rebecca and George Latimer's four children. Both George and Rebecca were runaway slaves who fled from the estate of James B. Gray in Virginia to Boston, Massachusetts, in 1842. When Gray came to Boston to recapture Rebecca and George, the court case established to defend their freedom, supported by William Lloyd Garrison, became a major precedent supporting the abolition of slavery. Lewis Latimer joined the Navy when he was 15 years old and was honorably discharged two years later.

After his service in the Navy, Latimer got a job at a law firm that focused on patent law where he learned to use a set square, ruler, and other drafting tools. His aptitude for drafting was noticed by his boss, who eventually promoted Latimer to head draftsman in the office by 1872. In 1874, Latimer and fellow-inventor Charles Brown patented an updated toilet for railcars. Latimer's work at the law office taught him how to submit patents to the U.S. patent office, and in 1876, Latimer was hired by Alexander Graham Bell to draft the patent needed for Bell's new invention, the telephone. Latimer became a central figure in the electric illumination of the country when he invented a carbon-filament light bulb for Hiram Maxim's U.S. Electric Lighting Company. Latimer's filament was much more durable than those in Edison's lightbulbs. He received a patent for his invention in 1881.

A few years later, Latimer was hired by Edison himself to work at the Edison Electric Light Company in New York, where he worked as a draftsmen and witness to the litigation proceedings over the patents of electric lights at the time. Latimer oversaw the installation of electric light utilities in New York, Philadelphia, Montreal, and London. Latimer continued to work for Edison when General Electric was founded after Edison Electric merged with Thomson-Houston Electric Company in 1892. From 1903 until his death in 1928, he lived on Holly Avenue in Queens, New York, with his family. The house has been relocated to 137th Street.

Lewis Howard Latimer is an inductee of the National Inventors Hall of Fame for the improvements he made upon Edison's lightbulb by adding a more durable carbon filament.

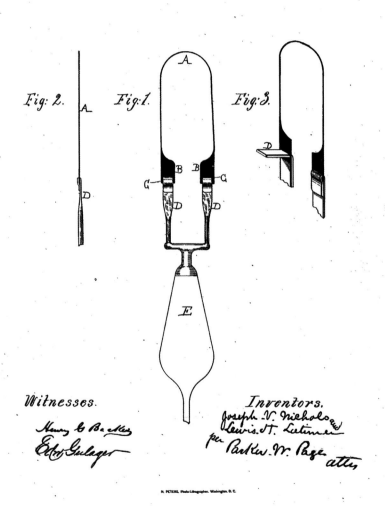

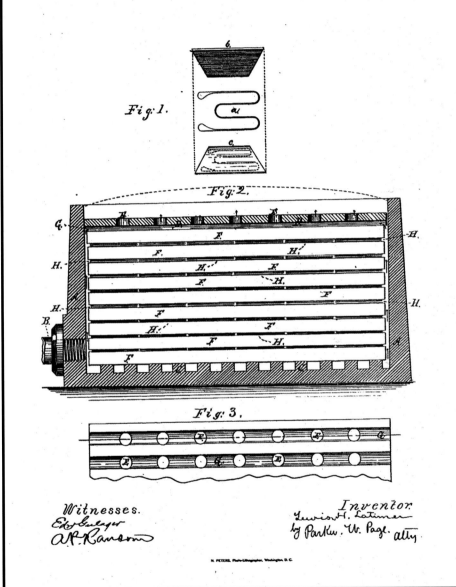

Latimer's patent for an electric lamp received in 1881.

Latimer's patent for the production of carbon filaments for his electric lamp received in 1882.

Alexander Graham Bell 1847–1922

Alexander Graham Bell was born in Edinburgh, Scotland, on March 3, 1847, to Alexander Melville Bell, a professor and phonetician, and Eliza Grace Bell. Alexander's brother, father, and grandfather all worked with elocution and speech, and his mother and wife were both deaf, all of which had a profound influence on Alexander's curiosity with sound and career as an inventor. Alexander began inventing at an early age, concocting a corn dehusking machine for a neighbor at age 12. He also had a propensity for music and poetry. His father published papers and lectured about techniques to teach deaf mutes to talk and lip read, and Alexander was so proficient in his father's techniques that he often accompanied his father to demonstrate his skills on stage. Bell attended the Royal High School in Edinburgh and received a student-teacher position in music and elocution at the Weston House Academy in Elgin, Scotland.

He was accepted to University College London, and the family moved to London, but Alexander soon fell sick from exhaustion. His brother also fell sick from tuberculosis, a disease from which he would never recover. Alexander recovered and left his studies behind to help his family by teaching deaf-mute students at Susanna Hull's private school in London. When he was 23 the family moved to Brantford, Ontario, Canada, and Alexander set up a workshop where he began working on his "harmonic telegraph," what would later become the telephone. Alexander and his father began travelling to Boston in order to teach at deaf schools in the area. Alexander moved to Boston and opened his own school in 1872 where he used his father's methods to teach deaf-mute students.

Alexander soon accepted a teaching position at Boston University as a professor of vocal physiology and elocution, but his dedication to his experiments with transferring sound with electricity soon led him to exhaustion and deteriorating health. He gave up his professorship and private practice and dedicated his time to developing transmitters and receivers for his harmonic telegraph. By 1875, Bell submitted his patent for the acoustic telegraph. His invention would change communication technology forever, connecting the United States and its disparate coasts in a time when the industrial market was wildly expanding. Alexander worked throughout his life on a number of devices whose technology would become ubiquitous in our modern world, including the metal detector, the phonograph, audiometers for hearing tests, solar panels, tape recorders, and photophones. Alexander died on August 2, 1922, after suffering from complications due to diabetes.

Alexander Graham Bell was a scientist and inventor who developed techniques of capturing and transferring sound with electricity, resulting in his invention of the telephone. He was also a teacher of deaf mutes and advanced the pedagogical fields that promoted their use of language.

Top: Alexander Graham Bell, seen at the top right of this photo, with the student body and faculty of the Boston School of Deaf Mutes in 1871.

Right: Alexander Graham Bell sends the first message over the long-distance telephone line between New York and Chicago in 1892.

Thomas Edison 1847–1931

Thomas Edison was born in Ohio in 1847. He developed hearing problems at a young age, either due to a case of scarlet fever or because he was struck by a train conductor when a laboratory on a boxcar he was working in set fire. He became a telegraph operator, working first for the Grand Trunk Railway and later for Western Union. He began his career as an inventor in 1877, and continued to be active in developing new commercial products right up until his death in 1931.

One of Edison's personal favorites among all of his inventions, the phonograph was also one of his first truly groundbreaking inventions. Edison's design used a needle that would vibrate when the user spoke into the receiver, causing it to make marks on a rotating drum wrapped in foil. Eventually, Edison would develop a phonograph that used discs and cylinders to allow music to be recorded—the forerunner of the record player. The first message Edison recorded was a recitation of the poem "Mary Had a Little Lamb." When he played it back, he and his staff were delighted by the invention's success.

Edison is probably best known for having invented the light bulb. This belief isn't precisely accurate, however: light bulbs had existed for several years before Edison's invention, but they were expensive, unreliable, and only lasted a few hours before they burned out. There was an ongoing race to perfect the electric light bulb when Edison took on the challenge.

His innovation was to create a vacuum inside the bulb, use a carbon filament, and reduce the voltage to make the bulb stable and long-lasting. His first success created a bulb that lasted for thirteen and a half hours. He later switched to using a carbonized bamboo filament. This bulb lasted over 1,200 hours.

Edison and the second model of his phonograph pictured in 1878.

Left: An illustration of Edison's first motion picture device, the kinetoscope, which was similar to the design of his phonograph. Thanks to George Eastman's invention of 35mm celluloid film, Edison was able to develop the strip kinetograph. The film, cut into long strips that were perforated along the edges, moved past a shutter, and the viewer observed twenty-second films through a peephole. Later, Edison manufactured and marketed Thomas Amat's vitascope, which was the first movie projector.

Right: Edison pictured in 1915. In 1906 Edison bought his birthplace in Milan, Ohio, and found, much to his surprise, that it was still lit by candlelight.

With the success of his light bulb, Edison realized that an electric distribution system was necessary to make it a commercially viable competitor with existing gas lighting utilities. In the 1880s he patented a system for distributing electricity and founded the Edison Illuminating Company. In January 1882, Edison's first steam-powered electric power station was turned on in London. It powered street lamps and a few houses close by. In September of that year his first generating station in the United States was switched on, providing 110 volts to 59 customers in lower Manhattan. And on January 19, 1883, the first incandescent electric streetlight system that used overhead wires was installed in Roselle, New Jersey. Edison died in at his home in West Orange, New Jersey, due to complications with diabetes in 1931. There is a sealed test tube at the Henry Ford Museum in Detroit that supposedly contains the last dying breath of Thomas Edison. A death mask was also made of Edison shortly after his death.

Nikola Tesla 1856–1943

Nikola Tesla was born on July 10, 1856, in the Serbian village of Smiljan, not far from the Adriatic Sea in what was then the Austrian Empire. His father, Milutin, was an Eastern Orthodox priest, and his mother, Duka, had the ability to memorize epic poems and create mechanical appliances although she never received a formal education. Nikola was greatly influenced by his mother's creative ability and claimed that much of his talent and intelligence came from her and her genetics. After receiving primary schooling from various schools, Nikola contracted cholera and approached death many times during the sickness. He recovered, avoided conscription in the Austro-Hungarian Army by living in the mountains, and enrolled in Austria Polytechnic in Graz, Austria. He dropped out of school when he lost his money while gambling, but that would not stop him from finding a career in engineering.

In 1882, Nikola landed a job with the Continental Edison Company in Paris where he began installing electric lighting throughout the city. Management noticed Nikola's deep understanding of technical matters and soon had him re-engineering dynamos and motors. He also consulted in Germany and France on engineering problems. He emigrated to the U.S. in 1884 and began working at the Edison Machine Works in lower Manhattan. He only worked for Edison for six months before he quit to work on his own lighting system that used his alternating current (AC) system, as opposed to Edison's direct current (DC) system. The Tesla Electric Light & Manufacturing company was born. But investors were not interested in Tesla's mechanical developments, and they eventually abandoned the company to focus on creating an electric utility. Nikola was left penniless, but he was soon refunded and founded the Tesla Electric Company in 1887.

Nikola Tesla is an often forgotten inventor, scientist, and engineer of American history who revolutionized the use of electricity in the U.S. with his development of alternating current (AC) systems that rivaled Thomas Edison's direct current (DC) system.

Tesla in front of a coil he used for his experiments in wireless power. Tesla believed that electric power could be delivered to locations without wires with the use of electromagnetic waves.

Tesla holding a bulb illuminated by wireless power in his New York laboratory in the 1890s.

Tesla licensed the patent for his electric induction motor and transformer to Westinghouse Electric in 1888. Soon after, as the nation began building infrastructure for electric utilities, the War of Currents began between Edison and Tesla, and Westinghouse was no longer able to pay licensing fees to Tesla. Westinghouse bought Tesla's patent outright, making Tesla wealthy enough to set up his own laboratory to begin pursuing the use of the electromagnetic field for wireless communication and lighting. All the while, Tesla became an American citizen, and Westinghouse won the electric-lighting contract for Chicago's Columbian Exposition in 1893, putting Tesla's AC system on the map as the preeminent method of electrification. Tesla had won the War of Currents, but he lacked the financial backing to support further innovations that careened in his imagination. He spent the last years of his life leaving unpaid bills behind as he moved from one hotel to the next in New York. He died at the age of 84 in Room 3327 of the New Yorker Hotel on January 7, 1943.

Ralph Waldo Emerson 1803–1882

Ralph Waldo Emerson was born in Boston on May 25, 1803. He graduated from Harvard College in 1821 and attended the Harvard School of Divinity in 1824. In 1826, he travelled to South Carolina and Florida, where he first witnessed slavery, an experience that would stay with him his entire life.

Emerson travelled to Europe for a year, and while he was there he met William Wordsworth, Samuel Taylor Coleridge and other writers. Upon his return to America, he began giving talks about spirituality and living ethically, and published many of these lectures as essays. In 1834 he moved to Concord, and married Lydia Jackson the next year. In Concord he began spending time with a group of intellectuals that included Henry David Thoreau and Margaret Fuller.

Emerson's circle of friends eventually became known as the American Transcendentalists. They espoused a belief that one can move past, or transcend, the physical senses to acquire a deeper spiritual experience of the world. They believed that God was not a remote, enigmatic deity, but one who could be understood by introspection and exploration of one's place in the natural world.

Emerson soon became one of the leading figures of the Transcendentalist movement. He founded *The Dial,* a literary magazine, and published dozens of essays in the 1840s. One of his best known essays, "Self-Reliance," was published in 1841. It presented a discussion on one of his recurrent themes: the importance of resisting conformity and "foolish consistency," and the necessity of following one's own ideas. During the 1840s Emerson also wrote "Friendship" and "Experience," two well-known essays.

Emerson was a major figure in the movement of romanticism in American literature, stating that his work largely focused around "one doctrine, namely, the infinitude of the private man."

A photo of Lydia Jackson, whom Emerson married on September 14, 1835, and their son Edward Waldo Emerson pictured in 1850.

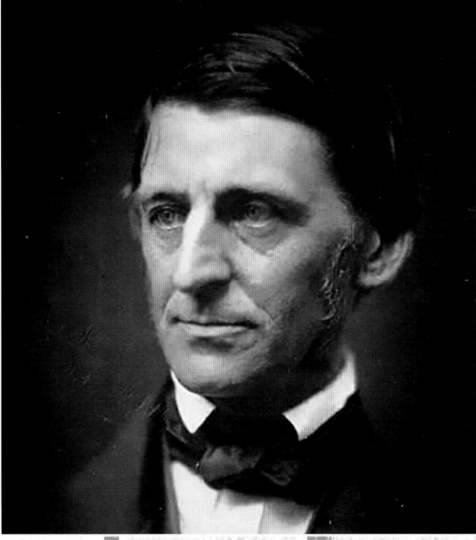

In his later years, Emerson began experiencing problems with his memory, aphasia, and general poor health. By the later 1870s, Emerson's memory problems were so bad that he often could not remember his own name. When asked how he felt, he often answered that although he lost his mental faculties he still felt quite well.

By 1860, Emerson's work began showing a more moderate philosophy that spoke of the importance of balancing individual nonconformity with social responsibility, which he discussed in "The Conduct of Life," published that year. In it, he tackled some of the difficult problems of the day, including the question of slavery. He argued that the Civil War would be necessary to ensure a rebirth of the nation, writing that "wars, fires, and plagues" destroy old institutions and allow society to recreate itself. He drew on the natural cycle of destruction preceding creation to support his position. He began advocating for the abolition of slavery in his lecture circuit in the 1860s. Following the Civil War, he toured less, and began to be referred to as "the Sage of Concord." He continued to write during the 1870s, and died in 1882 from pneumonia. He was buried in Sleepy Hollow Cemetery in Concord, Massachusetts.

Rachel Carson 1907–1964

Rachel Carson was born near Springdale, Pennsylvania, on May 27, 1907, to Maria and Robert Warden Carson. As a child she spent a lot of time exploring her family's 65-acre estate that was situated along the Allegheny River. She became a voracious reader and started composing her own short stories at a young age. She graduated from high school at the top of her class and soon began attending the Pennsylvania College for Women. She graduated *magna cum laude* in 1929 after studying biology and then continued her studies at Johns Hopkins. Upon graduating from Johns Hopkins with a degree in zoology, she obtained a job at the U.S. Fish and Wildlife Service where she wrote radio copy for the department.

She excelled at the U.S. Fish and Wildlife Service and was promoted many times. From writing radio copy to analyzing data of fish populations to becoming the chief editor of publications in the department, Carson received more and more liberty to research and write about what intrigued her. In 1937, she published her first book, *Under the Sea Wind*, which discussed life on the ocean floor and advanced her writing career. She began researching and publishing a series of articles in magazines like the *New Yorker, Science Digest*, and the *Yale Review* for her second book, *The Sea Around Us*, which was published in 1951 by Oxford University Press. The book won the National Book Award for Nonfiction and garnered Carson two honorary doctorates.

After the success of *The Sea Around Us*, Carson quit her job and began to focus solely on writing. She continued to write about aquatic ecosystems and their conservation, and then began to focus on the increased use of pesticides by the American government in the late 1950s. Carson's landmark publication, *Silent Spring*, was published in 1962 and described the harmful effects pesticides like DDT on the environment. The book helped launch a massive environmental movement in the U.S. due to its poetic language and stern representation of scientific facts. Carson argued that pesticides would weaken ecosystems, making them vulnerable to invasive species, while also creating pesticide-resistant bugs that would become harder and harder to manage. The book was a national success and had a profound influence on the rise of environmentalism and conservationism, but Carson died soon after its publication. Carson suffered from breast cancel and died on April 14, 1964, in Silver Springs, Maryland.

Rachel Carson was a writer, conservationist, and environmentalist who created a massive movement concerned for the health of our environment and its effects on the health of humanity with her book *Silent Spring*.

Top: Rachel Carson conducting research in 1952 after the publication of *The Sea Around Us*.

Bottom: Carson testified in front of the Science Advisory Committee organized by President Kennedy in 1963. The committee confirmed many of Carson's claims in their report published later that year.

W.E.B. Du Bois 1868–1963

William Edward Burghardt Du Bois was born in Great Barrington, Massachusetts, on February 23, 1868. He was able to attend school with white classmates, and his white teachers supported his academic studies. In 1885, he was accepted to Fisk University, a historically black college in Nashville, Tennessee. It was while he was in Nashville that Du Bois had his first encounters with Jim Crow laws and found himself treated as a second-class citizen. While he was at Fisk, he began developing a deep awareness of the viciousness of American racism.

After graduating from Fisk with a Bachelor's degree, he attended Harvard College from 1888-1890, where he graduated *cum laude* with a bachelor's in history. He supported himself with scholarships and summer jobs while he studied. He began a graduate program in sociology at Harvard in 1891, and he became the first African American to receive a Ph.D. from Harvard.

Du Bois published "Strivings of the Negro People" in 1897, an article that argued against Frederick Douglass' assertion that African Americans should integrate into white society. Instead, he wrote, African Americans should embrace their roots while striving to secure a place in American society. He gained national prominence when he spoke out against Booker T. Washington's Atlanta Compromise. The Atlanta Compromise proposed that African Americans in the South should submit to white rule, provided they were guaranteed education and economic opportunities. Dubois argued that African Americans were guaranteed equal rights by the 14th Amendment, and should fight for them.

In 1899, Du Bois published his findings in the first sociological case study of the African-American community, titled *The Philadelphia Negro: A Social Study*. His study found that racial segregation was a highly negative factor in social outcomes in African-American communities. In *The Philadelphia Negro*, Du Bois coined the term "the talented tenth," which he used to describe the probability of one in ten African-American men becoming leaders of their community.

Top: Du Bois helped organize the Silent Parade in 1917. The Silent Parade was a demonstration of 10,000 marchers against the violence perpetrated against the black population. The parade was inspired by another parade in May of that year in East St. Louis when 40 black men were killed by white mobs.

Bottom: A photo of the founders of the Niagara Movement, which fought against racial segregation, disenfranchisement, and the conciliatory and accommodating policies of Booker T. Washington. Du Bois is in the middle row in the white hat.

In 1903, Du Bois wrote *The Souls of Black Folk*, a collection of essays on race. In it, he argues that African Americans in the South deserve the right to vote, education, and equal treatment before the law. He also discusses his opposition to the Atlanta Compromise. Du Bois cofounded the National Association for the Advancement of Colored People (NAACP) in 1909, and edited *The Crisis*, its monthly publication. The NAACP challenged Jim Crow laws with test cases in the courts, and organized political opposition to segregation in marches. By 1920, the organization had nearly 90,000 members. W.E.B. Du Bois died on August 27, 1963, in Accra, Ghana. The next day, Dr. Martin Luther King Jr. delivered the iconic "I Have a Dream" speech at the March on Washington.

Mary Fields 1832–1914

Mary Fields was born into slavery in Tennessee. By the end of the Civil War, Mary (then in her 30s) had made her way to Ohio, where she found work at a Catholic mission school. Fields became close to a nun named Mother Amadeus. When Mother Amadeus was sent to Montana Territory in 1884 to help establish a mission school for Native American women, she brought along Mary to help.

St. Peter's Mission School was built near Cascade, about 60 miles north of Helena. Fields regularly drove a mission wagon into Cascade, loading up supplies and lumber with a cigar in her mouth. There were fewer than 350 African Americans in vast Montana Territory, and wary townspeople called her "Black Mary." Occasionally the strapping woman brawled with one or another of the employees. Once, Fields and an antagonist angrily went for their guns. No one was hit in the exchange of gunfire, but the bishop fired Fields. Mother Amadeus helped Fields open a restaurant in Cascade. She was a good cook, but twice she went out of business because she fed everyone regardless of their inclination to pay.

Her generosity, kindness, and independence won over the people of Cascade, and she became the first woman allowed to drink in the town's saloons. Friends helped her build a house in Cascade, and when it burned down, townspeople helped her rebuild it. "Black Mary" became "Stagecoach Mary" by riding shotgun and working as a driver on a local stagecoach line. When a mail route was established between Cascade and the mission, Fields was appointed carrier, becoming only the second woman in history to deliver U.S. mail.

Mary Fields was a stagecoach driver who stood six feet tall, smoked cigars, drank whiskey, never ducked a fight, and packed a .38 in addition to a double-barreled shotgun. She was an American pioneer.

Top: St. Peter's Mission pictured here in 1884. Mary Fields can be seen to the right sitting in her stagecoach.

Right: A portrait of Mother Amadeus who was a companion and supporter of Mary Fields.

Sarah Winnemucca 1844–1891

Sarah Winnemucca was born near Humboldt Lake, Nevada, in 1844, to a prominent Northern Paiute family. Her family tried to settle tensions between the Paiute and white settlers in the West in the mid-nineteenth century. She attended a Catholic school in Santa Clara, California, and during the Paiute War in 1860, her family moved away from their home in Paiute lands to San Francisco, California, and Virginia City, Nevada. Her family travelled the West, performing their "A Paiute Royal Family" on stage to make a living. All the while tensions in northern Paiute territory continued to escalate.

In 1865, the Northern Paiute tribe was attacked by U.S. Calvary in a skirmish that killed 29 Paiute members, including Sarah's mother and several other extended family members. The incident shook Sarah, and she soon began advocating for the rights of Native Americans throughout the nation. She wanted to increase the nation's awareness of the plight that had been placed upon Native American peoples by settlers and military forces. She worked as a translator and scout for the U.S. Army during the Bannock Wars, earning a good reputation with representatives from the U.S. government.

The Northern Paiutes were soon forced from their traditional territories and moved the Yakama Reservation in the late 1870s. The conditions at the reservation were horrid and the Northern Paiutes endured many hardships. Sarah accompanied the tribe as a translator to the new reservation, and then travelled to Washington, D.C., to petition the government to allow the Paiute to return to their territory. Her efforts were heard by Secretary of the Interior Carl Schurz, but he forced the Northern Paiutes to stay because the land to which they desired to return had already been developed. The Northern Paiutes subsequently had no place to return. Sarah began a lecturing series throughout the nation calling for the civil treatment of Native Americans. She died of tuberculosis in 1891 at her sister's home in Henry's Lake, Idaho.

Sarah Winnemucca was a Paiute activist who lectured for the rights of Native Americans in the late nineteenth century.

Top: : The Paiute tribe was separated into many bands and were very influential in the fight for Native American rights during the age of Western Expansion. The Ghost Dance religion, a Native American religious movement used to unite Native American tribes to resist white settlement, was founded by the Paiute spiritual leader Wovoka.

Bottom: : Sarah Winnemucca's father, Winnemucca the Younger, in a United States army uniform. He was a leader of the Paiute tribe and built canals and schools in their traditional territories.

Dr. Charles Eastman 1858–1939

Born on February 19, 1858, on the Santee Dakota Reservation near Redwood Falls, Minnesota, Charles Eastman's original name was Hakadah, meaning "pitiful last" due to his mother's death during his birth. Charles was separated from his father and brothers during the Dakota War of 1862 when he was taken by his maternal grandparents to flee toward North Dakota. Charles was reunited with his father and brothers many years later. By that time, his father had converted to Christianity and changed his name to Jacob Eastman; Charles also converted and changed his name to Charles Alexander Eastman. Jacob wanted his sons to receive an American education and sent Charles to study first at Knox College in Galesburg, Illinois, and Beloit College in Wisconsin to then graduate from Dartmouth in 1887. After graduating he attended medical school at Boston University, graduating as the first Native American to earn a degree in Western medicine in 1889.

Eastman began working for the Bureau of Indian Affairs as a physician on the Pine Ridge and Crow Creek Reservations in South Dakota. He treated many of the wounded Native Americans after the Wounded Knee Massacre in 1890, and began his own private practice that would eventually fail to make him and his family a living. Between the years of 1894 and 1897, Eastman began an active political career in which he founded several Native American groups for the YMCA, recruited children to attend the Carlisle Indian Industrial School in Pennsylvania, and lobbied for the Dakota. In 1903, he was appointed by President Roosevelt to help Sioux tribe members to anglicize their names in order to prevent them from losing their lands due to administrative confusion.

Eastman co-founded the Society of American Indians and became a committee member of the Committee of One Hundred, which looked at the treatment of Native Americans under U.S. administration. He suggested that the administration take an in-depth look at the health, education, and general livelihoods of Natives on reservations. The Committee eventually influenced President Roosevelt's New Deal for the Indian agenda that included the Indian Reorganization Act. In 1911, Eastman was selected to represent Native Americans at the Universal Races Congress in London where he spoke of harmonious living with nature and peace. Eastman died of a heart attack on January 8, 1939, in Detroit, Michigan.

Charles Eastman was a member of the Santee Sioux tribe, physician, and activist. He served as a bridge between two clashing cultures and helped ease the hardships that Native Americans suffered from white settlement in their territories.

Top: Charles Eastman was the first person to receive the American Indian Achievement Award in 1933.

Bottom: A photo of the delegates of the first Universal Races Congress held in London in 1911. Charles Eastman represented Native Americans at the conference.

Cesar Chavez 1927–1993

Cesar Chavez warn born in Yuma, Arizona, on March 31, 1927. His family owned a ranch and grocery store before the Great Depression but lost their property in the 1930s after the economic failure struck. His family then moved and worked in California's agricultural areas picking lettuce, cherries, corn, and beans. He dropped out of school in his early teens and never attended high school. Instead, he began full-time migrant farm work picking produce so his mother would not have to. In 1952, after working in the fields for many years, Chavez began organizing for the Latino civil-rights group Community Service Organization (CSO), where he registered Mexican-Americans to vote in California and petitioned for the rights of migrant farm workers. Cesar became the national director of the organization after meeting CSO co-founder Fred Ross, and then focused the organization's attention toward ending the abuses around agreements with Mexican-immigrant farm laborers.

After leaving the CSO in 1962, Cesar then co-founded the National Farm Workers Association, now the United Farm Workers (UFW), with labor leader Dolores Huerta. The UFW organized several Californian farm worker strikes in order to acquire a better rate of pay for them. These strikes led to other organized strikes throughout Texas and the Midwest, inspiring the foundation of two other labor-activist groups in Ohio and Wisconsin. During the 1970s Chavez also organized the largest farm workers strike in American history, the Salad Bowl Strikes, that led to boycotts of lettuce and grapes, hoping to impact the sales of those products enough to affect the growers' profit margins.

Cesar Chavez was a labor activist who fought for the rights of migrant farm workers throughout the nation, founding the United Farm Workers organization that spearheaded several boycotts and labor strikes throughout the mid-twentieth century.

Top: Chavez popularized the saying *Si Se Puede*, "Yes We Can," which was was used as a slogan in Barack Obama's 2008 presidential campaign.

Left: Chavez's nonviolent approach to labor rights gave the movement national attention.

Chavez became a very influential leader in Latino and Hispanic communities. He would often go on hunger strikes to support his initiatives, seeing it as his moral responsibility as a labor leader. Chavez and the UFW began to work in changing laws and the policies of California to support farm workers. He supported Jerry Brown and organized a march of a few hundred UFW leaders from San Francisco that ended with several thousand marchers joining by time the march reached Modesto. The march demonstrated the UFW's influence, and Brown began to support their initiatives, passing the California Agricultural Labor Relations Act to allow farm workers to organize and unionize. By the 1980s, Chavez organized more grape boycotts to protect workers from being exposed to pesticides that were used in the field. The bumper sticker campaign "NO GRAPES" garnered lots of attention but little legislative change occurred. Chavez died of unknown natural causes on April 23, 1993, that may have been caused from complications that arose after his last hunger strike during the "NO GRAPES" campaign.

Dolores Huerta 1930–

Dolores Huerta was born on April 10, 1930, in Dawson, New Mexico. As a child, her family moved around, and her parents worked as migrant farm workers. Her father would often talk of labor activism and unionization. Dolores's parents divorced when she was three. Dolores and her mother moved to Stockton, California. Dolores's activist ideals became apparent in high school, and after she graduated with a teaching degree from Stockton College, she began organizing and fighting for the labor rights of farm workers.

In the 1950s, she co-founded the Stockton chapter of the Community Service Organization (CSO) with Fred Ross in order to create economic opportunities for Latinos in her community. Dolores assumed large responsibilities in the organization and often encountered racism and discrimination due to the position and power she held as a woman of color. She co-founded the Agricultural Workers Association in 1962 and fought for legislation that would improve the living conditions of workers, and then went on to co-found the United Farm Workers with Cesar Chavez in 1962. Together they organized the Delano Grape Strike, and Dolores negotiated a three-year collective bargaining contract between the workers and the companies that controlled the grape industry.

Throughout her career, she fought for legislation that would permit Spanish speakers to take the California driving exam, repeal the Bracero Program, and extend family aid to migrant workers. She has remained active in many progressive movements throughout her lifetime and has been arrested dozens of times for civil disobedience and political demonstrations. In 1988 she was beaten by police during a demonstration. After her recovery, she took time away from labor activism and began focusing her attention on women's issues. She founded the Dolores Huerta Foundation in 2002 to support issues surrounding health, environment, youth development, and economic development.

Dolores Huerta is a labor activist who has fought for the rights of migrant farm workers, women, and the environment. She co-founded the United Farm Workers with Cesar Chavez in 1962 and was awarded the Presidential Medal of Freedom by President Barack Obama.

Dolores Huerta was the first Latina to be inducted into the National Women's Hall of Fame in 1993. She was also the honorary co-chair of the Women's March on Washington in January 2017.

Eugene V. Debs 1855–1926

Born in Terre Haute, Indiana, on November 5, 1855, Eugene V. Debs was the son of French immigrants. He attended public school until he dropped out when he was 14 to begin working in the railroad industry. He cleaned grease from railroad cars for 50 cents a day, eventually being promoted to paint the cars. A few years later, Debs became a railway fireman and joined the Brotherhood of Locomotive Fireman (BLF) in 1875, becoming more and more active in the organization and local politics. He edited the BLF's publication, served as the organization's secretary and treasurer, and eventually attained a Democratic seat on the Indiana General Assembly.

Debs pushed the BLF to become more active in labor efforts as railroads became more powerful companies. After the failed strike against the Burlington Railroad in 1888, Debs was convinced that stronger organization on the side of railway laborers was needed. He stepped away from the BLF and founded the American Railway Union (ARU), the first industrial union in the U.S., in 1893. He was elected the union's president after its founding and led the union to their first victory against the Great Northern Railway. In 1894, as the Pullman Palace Car Company, a leading railcar manufacturer at the time, began to cut workers' wages due to falling revenue, many ARU members who worked for the Pullman Company began to boycott handling any railcars made by Pullman. Debs was at first reluctant to support the strike due to high tensions between the workers, the Pullman Company, and the federal government, but Debs relented and the strike grew outside of Chicago, encompassing nearly 80,000 workers. Eventually, President Cleveland ordered the intervention of the army to break the strike, which led to the killing of nearly 30 workers and the blacklisting of several thousand workers. The strike is said to have cost nearly $80 million in property damage.

After the strike, Debs became a prominent Socialist leader, founding the Social Democrat party of the United States after the ARU dissolved. He ran for president of the United States as a Socialist party candidate five times in the early twentieth century, but to no avail. He went on to found the Industrial Workers of the World and continued his political activism and organizing. In 1918 he was arrested for ten counts of sedition after he spoke out against the military draft of World War I in Canton, Ohio. He was sentenced to ten years in prison but was released early. He died in 1926 due to a heart failure and is buried in Terre Haute, Indiana.

Eugene V. Debs was a socialist politician and labor activist who organized the Pullman Strike of 1894 and ran for president of the United States for the Socialist Democrat party five times.

Top: Debs speaking in Canton, Ohio, in 1918 during a speech renouncing the draft during World War I. The speech labeled him as a "traitor to his country" by President Woodrow Wilson. He was arrested and imprisoned for sedition after this speech.

Right: A photo from the Pullman Strike of 1894. Here we can see the U.S. Army in formation in front of a group of strikers protesting the Pullman Company cutting their wages.

Samuel Gompers 1850–1924

Samuel Gompers was born in London on January 27, 1850, to a very poor family. He attended a free Jewish school when he was six years old, where he learned to read and write. When he was thirteen, his family immigrated to the United States, settling in New York City. Gompers began working with his father as a cigar-maker. They joined the Cigar-Makers' Union, and Gompers quickly rose to a leadership position in the organization. He built the Union into a successful organization despite the advent of technological advances that could threaten cigar-makers' jobs.

In 1881, Gompers helped organize an informal association of several unions in order to promote collective bargaining across trades. In 1886, the loose affiliation was formally organized into the American Federation of Labor (AFL). Gompers became its president, and was the first leader of a national union who encouraged using strikes as an effective weapon to put pressure on employers. He was vehemently opposed to the Socialist faction within the AFL, believing that they acted toward political ends rather than toward securing conditions from employers. An immigrant himself, he opposed open immigration from Europe for fear that it would lower wages in the United States. He supported the U.S. invasion of Cuba during the Spanish Civil War, believing that it would improve conditions of cigar-makers there. After a long illness, Gompers died on December 13, 1924, in San Antonio, Texas.

Samuel Gompers was one of the most significant leaders of the early labor movement. He cofounded and was the first president of the American Federation of Labor. He was re-elected as the president for every year following, except one, until he died in 1924.

Top: The AFL used its efforts under the leadership of Gompers to help merge separate unions in the same field, act as a mediator to consolidate affiliated unions, and help consolidate unions to further fortify the strength of unions against corporations.

Left: Gompers pictured with Robert La Follette, a Progressive party presidential hopeful in the 1924 election, who campaigned for the end of child labor, the nationalization of the nation's railway utilities, the protection of civil liberties, and the end of American imperialism in Central America. He wanted to "break the combined power of the private monopoly system over the political and economic life of the American people."

Joe Hill 1879–1915

Joe Hill was born in Sweden on October 7, 1879. Both of his parents had died by time Joe was in his early twenties, and when he was 23, he emigrated to the U.S. with his brother where he became a laborer that traveled the country. Working his way from New York to Cleveland to San Francisco, Hill became a member of the International Workers of the World (IWW) while he was working at the docks of San Pedro, California. Hill was a singer and songwriter and wrote songs about activism, labor rights, and unionization. He quickly rose through the ranks of the IWW and traveled across the country to recruit new members for the organization.

In 1914, Joe Hill was suspected of killing a local grocery store clerk in Salt Lake City during a robbery he had purportedly been a part of. Suspicions began when Joe Hill arrived at a doctor's home with a gunshot wound the same night the grocer had been killed. Hill claimed that he was shot over a dispute he had with another man over a woman, but the gunshot was evidence enough for prosecutors to charge Hill for the murder of the grocer.

Hill was sentenced to death in a highly controversial trial at the time, and his defense attorneys claimed that Hill was found to be guilty because of his association with the IWW. Although Hill tried to keep his radical associations out of the trial, the press was eager to report on such issues. After appeals, public speeches against Hill's incarceration, and IWW movements to acquit Hill of the charges, Hill was executed by firing squad in 1915. Many say that Hill was a martyr for the labor rights movement, and that he was executed for being a socialist songwriter who incited instability in the country. His body was cremated, and his ashes were placed in 600 envelopes that were distributed throughout the world in 1917.

Joe Hill was born in Sweden and moved to America in his early twenties. He would later become an influential member of the IWW.

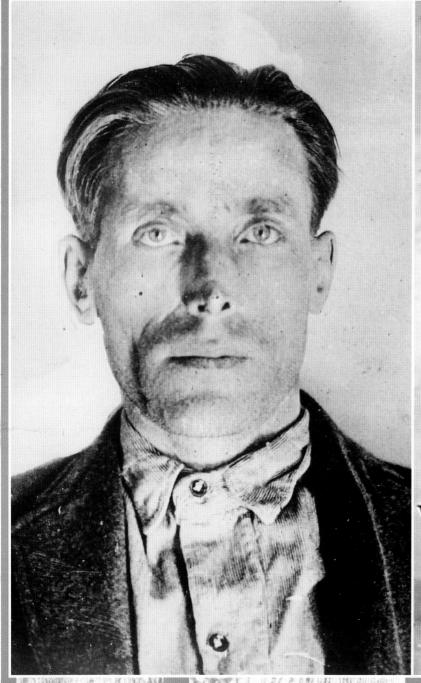

Joe Hill was a labor activist and member of the International Workers of the World, who was executed by firing squad after he was falsely convicted for murder. It is often thought that Hill was incarcerated and executed because of his ties with the IWW and his political activism.

Hill's song "The Rebel Girl" was inspired by the life of fellow IWW member Elizabeth Gurley Flynn.

William Green 1873–1952

William Green was the son of Welsh immigrants who worked in the coal mines near Coshocton, Ohio. By the time he was 16 years old, Green was working in the coal mines as well. He became a member of the Coshocton Progressive Miners Union soon after he began mining and ascended in the union's ranks. He was elected secretary of the union by the time he was 18, went on to become the union's subdistrict president, and then became president of the union's Ohio chapter in 1906.

Green's activity within the union, which had become the United Mine Workers of America (UMWA), soon led him to become a member of the Ohio Senate. As a senator, he supported many Progressive Era legislative acts that would enact limited work hours for women, popular-vote elections of Ohio senators, non-partisan run elections, and a one percent income tax. As a senator, he continued his service in the UMWA, gaining higher positions in the organization's ranks as the union's international statistician and then secretary-treasurer in 1913.

In 1916, Green became the chief council for the American Federation of Labor (AFL) and then became the AFL's president after the death of its former president, Samuel Gompers. During his time as president of the AFL, he served on President Roosevelt's Labor Advisory Council and National Labor Board. He worked for higher wages of all workers in the nation by promoting mutual self-interest between companies and employees, showing that productivity would go up if the workers felt like they were supported and respected by their employers. He also fought to restrict the number of hours workers worked in order to increase their standards of living and engagement in civil duties. Green died on November 21, 1952, and is buried at South Lawn Cemetery in Coshocton, Ohio.

William Green served as president of the AFL from 1924 to 1952.

Top: William Green was a labor activist and served as president of the American Federation of Labor (AFL). He used legislation to fight for the rights of workers to collectively bargain and collect unemployment insurance. He facilitated the passage of the National Labors Relation Act, the Fair Labor Standards Act, and the Norris-La Guardia Act. He was also one of five delegates to represent the U.S. at the Paris Peace Conference at the end of World War I.

Left: WIlliam Green began his career as a coal miner in Ohio, later becoming affiliated with mining unions at the local and national level.

Sidney Hillman 1887–1946

Sidney Hillman was born in Lithuania on March 23, 1887. As a child he showed great promise for his skills in academia, being able to memorize lengthy tracts of text. He was expected to study to become a rabbi as his father and grandfather had done. At the age of 13, he neglected his religious studies and began attending classes of an illegal study circle where he studied radical texts by Charles Darwin, Karl Marx, and John Stuart Mill. The classes led to his membership in the Bund, a socialist group of Jewish workers in the Russian Empire, where he would eventually participate in the 1905 Russian Revolution. As the tsar of the Russian Empire began intense raids and repressive campaigns against Socialist Russians, Hillman emigrated to the United Kingdom in 1906 and then to Chicago in 1907.

Hillman arrived in America in August of 1907. His job prospects in New York were not great, so he decided to move to Chicago where he hoped for better prospects. After a few years of various jobs, Hillman attained a job as an apprentice garment cutter. In 1910, Hillman organized a strike of nearly 45,000 women garment workers in the city. The strike was highly divisive and had strikers not only fighting against their employers but their own labor union, the United Garment Workers. Hillman led the workers to form the Amalgamated Clothing Workers of America (ACWA) and served as the union's president.

By the 1920s, Hillman and the ACWA had established programs of social unionism by offering low-income cooperative housing and unemployment insurance for its members. The ACWA also established their own bank to provide members with financial backing. Hillman worked as president to insure safe workplace conditions, livable wages, and manageable hours, believing that stability was the best way to build better workplace relationships. Hillman founded the American Labor party, vehemently opposed Nazi Germany, and worked as the leader of the labor division of the War Production Board during World War II. Hillman died on July 10, 1946, from a heart attack and is buried at the Westchester Cemetery in New York.

Sidney Hillman served on multiple war-time administrations during World War II, including the Office of Production Management, the Supply Priorities and Allocations Board, and Labor Division of the Office of Production Management.

Top: Sidney Hillman was a labor leader in the early twentieth century. He was the head of the Amalgamated Clothing Workers of America and was a key proponent in the formation of the Congress of Industrial Organizations, a federation of unions that wanted to organize industrial workers from various trades.

Bottom: A publicity photo for the Amalgamated Clothing Workers of America of their young president in 1922.

John L. Lewis 1880–1969

John L. Lewis was born in Cleveland, Iowa, on February 12,1880, to Thomas and Ann Walkins Lewis. His family belonged to the Reorganized Church of Jesus Christ of Latter Day Saints, and the church helped instill Lewis's beliefs of temperance, abstinence, and social support for the poor. He attended three years of high school in Des Moines and then began to work at the Big Hill Mine in Lucas, Iowa, at the age of 17. Lewis quickly became a member of the United Mine Workers (UMW), and by 1909 Lewis was elected president of the local chapter of the UMW in Panama, Illinois. Two years later, Lewis met UMW president Samuel Gompers, who promoted Lewis to the position of union organizer. Lewis travelled throughout the coal and steel districts of the Midwest to organize laborers.

Lewis spent several more years rising through the ranks of the UMW, and he eventually became the president of the union in 1920 after he organized the nation's first major coal strike of some 400,000 miners. As president, Lewis fought to keep the traditionally socialist-leaning UMW local chapters from being infiltrated by communist organizers. He would expel many of his political rivals from the ranks of the UMW, and exploit the nation's dependence on coal in order to attain higher wages and safer conditions for his miners.

Lewis and the members of the UMW supported Franklin Roosevelt during his first presidential campaign, and Roosevelt's New Deal programs in turn helped the UMW secure higher prices for coal and higher wages for miners. In 1935, Lewis began organizing laborers in many different industries and formed the Congress of Industrial Organizations (CIO). The CIO gained large amounts of members from the rubber, meat, steel, auto, glass, and electrical equipment industries and eventually established contracts with General Motors and United States Steel regarding collective bargaining. He continued to serve as the president of the CIO until 1940 and president of the UMW until 1960. He might have been a competitive and cutthroat leader that had no problem in ousting his rivals, but Lewis ensured fair compensation and safe workplaces for his members. He died on June 11, 1969, in Alexandria, Virginia, and is buried at Oak Ridge Cemetery, in Springfield, Illinois.

John L. Lewis was a labor leader who served as president of the United Mine Workers of America for many decades. He was awarded the Presidential Medal of Freedom by President Johnson and the Eugene V. Debs Award for his efforts to support industrial unionism.

Top: Lewis, on the right, pictured with UMW Secretary-Treasurer Thomas Kennedy, on the left, and UMW District 17 president Pery Tetlow during a conference of the National War Labor Board in 1943. The National War Labor Board was initiated during World War II to help manage labor disputes and shortages during the war.

Right: In 1952, John L. Lewis fought to pass the first Federal Mine Safety Act and tried to bolster the industry with new collective bargaining contracts. But by that time, the UMW had suffered many setbacks due to declining membership, mechanization of the industry, and growing non-union operations.

Louis Tikas 1886–1914

Louis Tikas was born on the island of Crete in 1886. Information about his childhood is unknown, but Tikas emigrated to the United States in 1910. After emigrating to the U.S., he moved to Denver, Colorado, where he opened a Greek coffee shop on Market Street. Tikas also worked as a mining strikebreaker, until he and several other Greek miners organized their own strike and walked out of the mine in Frederick, Colorado. During this walkout, he was shot by Baldwin-Felts detectives and barely escaped with his life by fleeing through the back door of the boarding house he was staying at. In 1912, Tikas was recruited by the United Mine Workers of America (UMWA) as a labor organizer, and in 1914 he led Colorado miners on a strike that would result in the Ludlow Massacre, a confrontation between Colorado miners and the Colorado National Guard that resulted in the killing of 19 people.

Many years before the strike, Tikas and the UMWA secretly began to organize miners who worked under the harsh conditions of the Colorado Fuel & Iron Company, which actively managed strikebreakers and dissolved any movements toward unionization. Tikas and UMWA presented the Colorado Fuel & Iron Company with a list of demands for the miners that called for the recognition of the union as a bargaining agent, an eight-hour work day, payment for work that was necessary outside of the mining itself, and the right to choose their own places to live. Many of the miners lived in company towns and were beholden to the regulations the company put upon their living situations. The demands were ignored by the company, and many of the miners who began to strike were evicted from their homes in the company town of Ludlow, Colorado. They moved to tent encampments that were set up by the union and continued their strike. Soon strikebreakers were sent in along with agents from the Baldwin-Felts Detective Agency to protect the strikebreakers and harass the strikers.

Top: Louis Tikas was a labor organizer that led miners in Colorado to strike against the Colorado Fuel & Iron Company. He died during the Ludlow Massacre.

Bottom: Pictured here are armed strikers and members of the United Mine Workers. The strikers were unsuccessful in attaining their demands and the union was never recognized by the Colorado Fuel & Iron Company.

The remains of the union camp near Ludlow, Colorado, after it was burned by the Colorado National Guard in 1914.

Tikas led the camp of nearly 1,200 strikers to persevere for nearly a year as they fought for better labor conditions. The Colorado National Guard was sent in to monitor and break the strike, and their efforts were successful. The Colorado Fuel & Iron Company continued production while the striking, unionized miners faced increasing threats of violence. On the morning of April 20, 1914, the Colorado National Guard demanded the release of a prisoner they accused the strikers of holding. Tikas went to negotiate with Major Pat Hamrock, but Hamrock was not looking to negotiate and prepared a military operation against the strikers. Later that day, the Colorado National Guard opened fire on the camp with machine guns and set the camp on fire. Tikas was captured and shot in the back. The massacre left two women, eleven children, and six others dead and became a rallying cry for strikers to fight back. In retaliation, a number of battles against the Colorado National Guard were initiated by the strikers in what would become known as the Colorado Coalfield War.

A. Philip Randolph 1889–1979

Born in Crescent City, Florida, on April 15, 1889, A. Philip Randolph was the second son of Methodist minister and tailor James William and seamstress Elizabeth Robinson. His family moved to Jacksonville, Florida, when he was still an infant. Randoph attended the Cookman Institute for his high-school education and graduated as valedictorian of his class. After graduation, he worked various jobs and became highly influenced by the writings of W.E.B. Du Bois, coming to believe that the fight for civil rights for African Americans was one of the most important initiatives to be pursued at the time. He moved to New York City in 1911 to escape from the lack of opportunity he found in the South and soon began taking classes at New York's City Colleges.

In New York, Randolph was exposed to the ideas of socialism and began collaborating with Chandler Owen, a Columbia University law student, to lessen the economic burdens of African Americans. Randolph came to believe that collective action was one of the best methods to attain civil rights. In 1917, Randolph began organizing elevator operators to unionize and then became president of the National Brotherhood of Workers of America until it was dissolved in 1921. Four years later, he was elected to become president of the Brotherhood of Sleeping Car Porters, which was one of the first unions supporting employees of the Pullman Car Company. Randolph continued to recruit Pullman employees to the Brotherhood of Sleeping Car Porters and began talk of a strike for better working conditions and pay.

A. Philip Randolph was a labor and civil rights activist who negotiated better working conditions at the Pullman Company for members of the Brotherhood of Sleeping Car Porters. He also helped organize the March on Washington for Jobs and Freedom.

A. Philip Randolph, seated in the center, with other organizers of the March on Washington for Jobs and Freedom at the Lincoln Memorial.

A. Philip Randolph receiving the Presidential Medal of Freedom in 1964 from President Johnson.

By 1932, President Franklin Roosevelt passed the Railway Labor Act which granted porters larger workplace rights, and the Pullman Company then began negotiating with the Brotherhood of Sleeping Car Porters. The union attained nearly $2,000,000 in pay increases, shorter work weeks, and pay for overtime work. With Randolph's successful negotiations for the union, he became a notable proponent of civil rights in the nation. He and other civil rights activists, such as Bayard Rustin, began to organize marches throughout the nation to protest the unequal treatment of African Americans. By the 1950s, Randolph and Rustin had begun to work with Martin Luther King Jr. to continue organizing marches, including the Prayer Pilgrimage for Freedom and Youth Marches for Integrated Schools. In 1963, Randolph helped organize the March on Washington for Jobs and Freedom, which brought together nearly 300,000 marchers to the nation's capital. A year later, the Civil Rights Act was passed by President Johnson. Randolph died on May 16, 1979, from a heart attack in his Manhattan apartment.

Sojourner Truth 1797–1883

Truth was born into slavery as Isabella Baumfree in 1797, in a Dutch enclave in upstate New York. She was sold around age 9 for $100 (which also included a flock of sheep) and endured physical abuse at the hands of her new master because she spoke limited English, her first language being Dutch. It was during this period that Truth first sought solace in religion, praying loudly whenever she was frightened or hurt.

Truth was sold several more times in the ensuing years. She married another slave in 1817 and bore four children. Freedom seemed at hand when the State of New York enacted legislation that called for the end of slavery within the state on July 4, 1827. Her owner promised to set her free a year early, but he reneged at the last minute. Angry and bitter at being lied to, Truth worked until she felt she had paid off her debt then walked away. She arrived at the home of Isaac and Maria Van Wagenen, who agreed to buy her services for the rest of the year for $20. The Van Wagenens treated Truth well and insisted she call them by their given names. It was while working for the Van Wagenens that Truth experienced a religious epiphany that inspired her to become a preacher.

Truth moved to New York City, where she decided to become a traveling minister. She changed her name from Isabella Baumfree to Sojourner Truth and set out on the road, relying on the kindness of strangers to make her way. In 1844, Truth joined a Massachusetts commune known as the Northampton Association of Education and Industry, which had been founded by a group of abolitionists who espoused women's rights and religious tolerance. She left when the collective disbanded in 1846.

Truth was very active during the Civil War, enlisting black troops for the Union and helping runaway slaves. In 1864, she worked at a government refugee camp for freed slaves on an island off the coast of Virginia, and she even met President Abraham Lincoln. Following the war, she continued her efforts to help newly freed slaves through the Freedman's Relief Association.

HOUSE OF COL. JOHANNES HARDENBERGH.

I Sell the Shadow to Support the Substance.

SOJOURNER TRUTH.

Truth began dictating her autobiography, *The Narrative of Sojourner Truth: A Northern Slave*, shortly after, and renowned abolitionist William Lloyd Garrison privately published the book in 1850. The memoir was a success and brought Truth both a needed income and promotion as a public speaker. Soon, Truth found herself in great demand, speaking about women's rights and the evils of slavery, often turning to her own experiences as illustration. In 1854, she gave one of her most famous lectures, titled "Ain't I A Woman?" at the Ohio Woman's Rights Convention in Akron.

Truth pursued her work on behalf of freed blacks until her death on November 26, 1883, from complications related to leg ulcers. She was buried next to her grandson, Sammy Banks, in Oak Hill Cemetery in Battle Creek, Michigan.

Left: The estate of Col. Hardenbergh in Esopus, New York, where Truth was enslaved up to the age of nine before she was sold to another slave owner in the area of Kingston, New York.

Right: Sojourner Truth's legacy of spiritual pursuit and social activism resulted in numerous honors in the decades following her death. Among them were a memorial stone in the Stone History Tower in downtown Battle Creek; a portion of Michigan state highway M-66 designated the Sojourner Truth Memorial Highway; induction into the national Women's Hall of Fame in Seneca Falls, New York; and a commemorative postage stamp.

Clara Barton 1821–1912

Clara Barton quit a teaching career after she discovered she couldn't earn the same pay men did. She was the first woman ever hired by the U.S. Patent Office in Washington, D.C., but although they hired her as a "clerk," they later dropped her title to "copyist" and paid her a mere 10 cents for every 100 words she copied. The Civil War allowed her true talents to come to the fore. In her free time, Barton had begun tending to wounded soldiers in the hospital. She quickly recognized the Army Medical Department's inability to care properly for so many casualties. At the time of the First Battle of Bull Run, the Union army had practically nothing in terms of a hospital corps. Taking on the daunting task herself, Barton placed an ad in a Massachusetts newspaper for donations of medical supplies. Ultimately, she founded an organization to collect and distribute provisions for wounded soldiers. Cutting through official red tape, Barton won permission from the War Department to go out into the field and help the wounded.

She began personally delivering critical supplies to battlefields where they were most needed. In August 1862, Barton witnessed firsthand the chaos, inefficiency, and unsanitary nature of military medical care during combat. The worst of these must have been Antietam, where on September 17, 1862—during the war's bloodiest single day of fighting—23,000 combatants were killed, wounded, or missing.

Barton died in 1912 from pnuemonia.

110

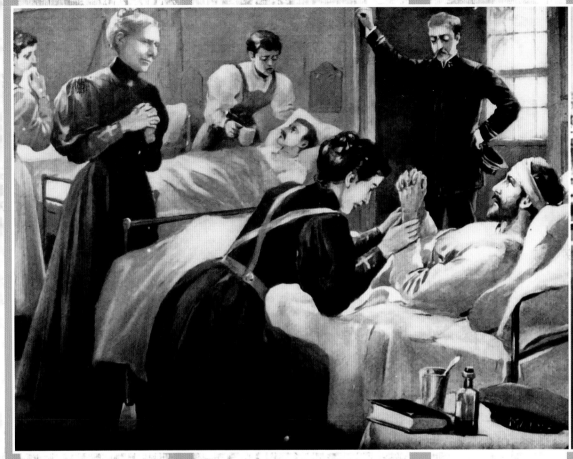

Illustration of Barton tending to a patient during the war.

Barton remained busy as a lecturer and activist after the war, campaigning for women's suffrage.

Dead and dying soldiers lay in heaps, while frantic doctors were reduced to binding wounds with cornhusks. Like an answered prayer, Clara Barton arrived with an entire wagonload of bandages. She dove into the fray, the only woman on the field, and indeed, the work was harrowing. At one point a soldier begged her to cut a bullet from his cheek. She hesitated, as she had no surgical instruments and was not a doctor. But the young man pleaded with her. She ended up cutting the bullet out with a pocketknife! As she cradled another wounded soldier in her arms to give him water, a bullet zipped past her, tearing the sleeve of her dress and killing the man she was helping. Rather than relent, she set upon creating a makeshift field hospital in a barn. When a surgeon she was assisting was suddenly killed, Barton took his place at the operating table. Barton saved the day again by seeking out lanterns and bringing several herself. She worked all through the night until she collapsed and was carried exhausted off the field.

Establishing the Office of Correspondence, Barton helped families learn the fate of nearly 30,000 soldiers missing in action. On her return home, Barton performed her most lasting act on behalf of suffering peoples everywhere—she founded the American Red Cross. In a sense, whenever we turn on the television today and see the Red Cross providing assistance after natural disasters, we are looking at Clara Barton's shining monument.

Mother Jones 1837–1930

Mary Harris Jones was born on May 1, 1837, in Cork, Ireland. She and her family were victims of the Great Famine of Ireland and emigrated to Canada when Mary was ten years old. Mary began her education at the Toronto Normal School when they arrived in Canada, and although she did not graduate, she did receive enough of a certification to attain a teaching position in Monroe, Michigan, after she left. She taught for some time and then moved to Chicago and later to Memphis, where she met her husband, George E. Jones, a member of and organizer for the National Union of Iron Moulders. After her marriage, Mary quit teaching and began housekeeping. In 1867, her husband and four children all died from a yellow-fever outbreak in Memphis, and Mary then decided to start a new life back in Chicago by opening a dressmaking shop.

Tragedy struck again in Mary's life when the Chicago Fire ravaged the city, including Mary's dressmaking shop and home. After the fire, she began organizing for the Knights of Labor, a labor federation that sought to uplift the working class with the ideals of republicanism. She organized strikes that often failed or ended in police suppression, and the Knights of Labor was dissolved as the fear of anarchism around labor organizations grew after the Haymarket Riot. She then joined the United Mine Workers (UMW), organizing strikes and supporting strikers when management brought in strikebreakers. By the end of the century, Mary Jones began referring to herself as Mother Jones, becoming a figurehead for the working class.

In 1901, she raised awareness throughout the nation of children working in horrid silk mill conditions. She organized the March of the Mill Children, where children who worked in silk mills marched to the hometown of President Theodore Roosevelt with signs that read, "We want to go to school and not the mines!" Mother Jones helped miners in West Virginia and soon faced a court martial for conspiring to commit murder due to the violence that broke out during the West Virginia strikes. She was sentenced to 20 years, but only served 85 days. After her release she went to Colorado to organize miners striking during the Colorado Coalfield War. She was arrested once again for her activities, but after her release and after the Ludlow Massacre, she was able to meet with coal-mine owner and industrialist John D. Rockefeller Jr. She helped convince Rockefeller to introduce long-sought reforms in his Colorado mines. Mother Jones died on November 30, 1930, at the age of 93 in Silver Springs, Maryland. She is buried at Union Miners Cemetery in Mount Olive, Illinois.

Mother Jones was a labor activist who organized strikes for the United Mine Workers. She was arrested several times for her activities but continued to fight throughout her life for the working class.

Top: Mother Jones speaking in 1912 at the Paint Creek-Coal Creek strike in West Virginia. She was arrested after martial law came into effect during the strike.

Right: Mother Jones differed from many other nineteenth-century female activists because she promoted many ideals other than women's suffrage. She is quoted in saying, "You don't need the vote to raise hell." When she was criticized for supposedly being against the right of women to vote, she would counter by saying that she was not against anything that promoted freedom. She believed the liberation of the working class to be the most important objective of her day.

John Brown 1800–1859

John Brown was born on May 9, 1800, in Torrington, Connecticut. His father, a Calvinist minister, taught him at a young age to support abolition. The lesson was seared into Brown's memory when he was twelve years old and witnessed the beating of a young African-American boy. Brown initially studied to be a minister, but instead became a tanner. His family moved around in his twenties and held different jobs.

In 1837, when the abolitionist Elijah Lovejoy was murdered, Brown swore to give his life to the abolitionist cause. He founded the League of Gileadites, an armed group that protected African Americans from slave catchers. In 1847 he met with Frederick Douglass. When the Kansas-Nebraska Act passed in 1854, Brown and five of his sons moved to Kansas to fight in the conflict over whether the state would be free or slave-owning territory. They killed five pro-slavery settlers in 1856.

In 1858, Brown freed a group of slaves from a Missouri farm and led them to freedom in Canada. He spent much of that year and the spring and summer of 1859 making preparations for the raid on Harpers Ferry. He gathered rifles, pikes and ammunition, and organized a group of 21 men. He discussed the raid with Harriet Tubman, who thought it was doomed to failure. On October 16, 1859, Brown and his men attacked the federal armory at Harpers Ferry and held it for two days before they were overwhelmed by federal troops led by Robert E. Lee. Brown was captured and convicted of treason. On December 2, 1859, he was executed. He became a symbol of the abolitionist movement, and during the Civil War Union troops sang "John Brown's Body" as they marched into battle.

"These men are all talk; What is needed is action–action!" –John Brown

Top: A *Harper's Weekly* illustration of the raid on John Brown's Fort in Harper's Ferry.

Left: A daguerreotype of John Brown taken by the African-American photographer Augustus Washington. The flag Brown is holding is the flag of the Subterranean Pass Way, which was Brown's militant group that was aligned with the Underground Railroad.

Susan B. Anthony 1820–1906

Born in Adams, Massachusetts, on February 15, 1820, Susan B. Anthony was the second of Daniel and Lucy Mead Anthony's seven children. Her family practiced the Quaker faith and believed in many radical views for the time. Her father supported abolition and the temperance movement. Two of her brothers, Daniel and Merritt, travelled to Kansas to support anti-slavery movements in the state. Susan attended a Quaker boarding school when she was 17, but she had to end her studies early due to financial problems that struck her family during the Panic of 1837. The family then moved to a farm on the outskirts of Rochester, New York, where the family associated with Quaker social reformers. The Anthony homestead became a meeting place for activists, and Anthony met many activists including Frederick Douglass.

As Anthony grew older, she became more active in radical movements, reading the works of William Lloyd Garrison and Elizabeth Cady Stanton, the organizer of the Seneca Falls Convention in 1848. Anthony met Stanton in 1851, and the two began a lifelong career working together for women's suffrage and the abolition of slavery. Together they founded the New York Women's State Temperance Society, the Women's Loyal National League, the American Equal Rights Association, National Woman Suffrage Association. In 1868, the two began publishing *The Revolution*, a newspaper focused on the issues of women's suffrage. Anthony faced criminal charges in 1872 after she attempted to vote in Rochester, New York. The court proceedings became widely publicized, but authorities did not push for her conviction.

Susan B. Anthony was an activist for the rights of women and African Americans in the mid-nineteenth century. Her activism helped lead to the passage of the 13th and 19th Amendments of the United States Constitution.

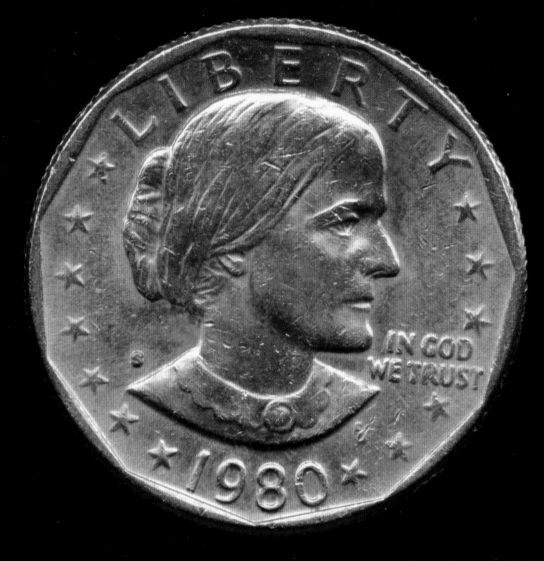

Left: A photo of Susan B. Anthony and Elizabeth Cady Stanton.

Right: Susan B. Anthony was the first historical woman to have her portrait depicted on U.S. coinage on the 1979 dollar coin.

Anthony travelled prolifically, speaking and lecturing throughout the nation about women's suffrage. In 1878, Anthony and Stanton presented Congress with an amendment to the constitution that would allow women to vote; the amendment was not approved until 1920 when the 19th Amendment was ratified. She also worked for women's rights internationally by serving on the International Council of Women. Anthony died in Rochester, New York, in 1906 from heart failure and pneumonia.

Elizabeth Cady Stanton 1815–1902

Elizabeth Cady was born in Johnstown, New York, on November 12, 1815. She attended Emma Willard's Troy Female Seminary, graduating in 1832. She often visited the home of her cousin Gerrit Smith, a social reformer and abolitionist, and their discussions shaped her early ideas about abolition, temperance, and equal rights for women. In 1840, Cady married Henry Stanton, himself a social reformer. She kept her own last name, and the couple removed the word "obey" from their marriage vows. On their honeymoon, they travelled to London to attend the World's Anti-Slavery Convention.

At the Convention, the men in attendance voted to exclude the women from participating, and forced them to sit in a segregated section. Cady Stanton, along with other women in attendance, was outraged. She met with Lucretia Mott, and there the two discussed holding a worldwide convention on women's rights for the first time. Cady Stanton and Mott would remain friends and collaborators for the rest of their lives.

In 1848, their vision of a women's rights convention became reality at Seneca Falls, New York. At the convention, Cady Stanton pushed for the adoption of a resolution that declared obtaining suffrage for women was a key tenet of the women's rights movement. There was initial opposition to the resolution. Nevertheless she persisted, and with the support of Frederick Douglass and other attendees, it passed.

Elizabeth Cady Stanton was one of the founders of the women's rights movement. She called for the Seneca Falls Convention on women's rights, helped write the Convention's Declaration of Sentiments, and advocated for the vote as president of the National Woman Suffrage Association.

Stanton served as the National American Woman Suffrage Association's first president, a post she held for two years, after the merger of the American Woman Suffrage Association and the National Woman Suffrage Association.

Elizabeth Cady Stanton with Susan B. Anthony.

Cady Stanton worked on the cause of abolishing slavery during the Civil War, and afterwards she continued to work for women's rights. In 1868, she began publishing the weekly newspaper *Revolution* with Susan B. Anthony, and co-founded the National Woman Suffrage Association (NWSA) with Anthony in 1869.

Between 1881 and 1886, she worked with Anthony and Matilda Joslyn Gage on the first three volumes of the *History of Woman Suffrage*, and in 1895 she published the first volume of *The Woman's Bible*. Cady Stanton had long held that organized religion helped to prevent women from obtaining equal rights. The second volume was published in 1898. Elizabeth Cady Stanton died on October 26, 1902. Eighteen years later, on August 18, 1920, the 19th Amendment was passed, guaranteeing women the right to vote.

Margaret Sanger 1879–1966

Margaret Sanger was born Margaret Louise Higgins on September 14, 1879, in Corning, New York. She attended Claverack College and the Hudson River Institute, then studied nursing at White Plains Hospital. In 1902, she married architect William Sanger, and the couple and their three children eventually settled in Greenwich Village in New York City.

In the bohemian neighborhood, Sanger began to embrace feminism, and in 1912 wrote a series of scandalous (for the day) columns on sex education for the magazine *New York Call*. She also began working as a nurse in the slums on the East Side, frequently meeting women who had undergone back-alley abortions or attempted to self-terminate pregnancies, and Sanger was dismayed that these women had no access to contraception.

In 1914, Sanger began publishing a magazine called *The Woman Rebel*, which advocated for a woman's right to birth control; however, the information she provided was considered "obscene and immoral," and her distribution of the magazine was illegal. Sanger fled to England to avoid prosecution, returning to the U.S. after charges against her were dropped. But she didn't come back alone: Sanger smuggled diaphragms back into the country.

In 1916, Sanger opened a birth control clinic in Brooklyn—distributing some of the contraband diaphragms—and was arrested nine days later. But she scored a win when a court ultimately decided to allow doctors to prescribe birth control for medical reasons. Her case drew attention across the country, increasing support for legal birth control. Sanger founded the American Birth Control League in 1921, a precursor to the Planned Parenthood Federation of America. Her continued efforts led to a 1936 court ruling that made it legal to import contraceptive devices into the country, and she was instrumental in recruiting biologist Gregory Pincus to develop the first oral contraceptive.

Margaret Sanger was a birth control activist and sex educator. She founded organizations that would later become Planned Parenthood Federation of America.

Margaret Sanger and her sister leaving court after she was arrested for opening her birth control clinic in Brooklyn.

A photo of the Sanger Clinic that was located 46 Amber Street in Brooklyn.

Sandra Day O'Connor 1930–

Sandra Day O'Connor was born in El Paso, Texas, on March 26, 1930, and spent much of her childhood on a remote cattle ranch in Arizona, where she became adept at hunting, riding horses, and changing flat tires. The closest school was a 32-mile bus ride away.

After high school, O'Connor studied economics at Stanford University, and then attended the university's law school, graduating third in her class in 1952. Legal jobs for women were scarce at the time, so O'Connor worked for the county attorney of the San Mateo region—without pay—to gain experience. She was soon employed as the deputy county attorney.

After briefly moving overseas when her husband, John Jay O'Connor III, was drafted, the couple eventually settled in Maricopa County, Arizona. O'Connor worked in private practice, and then as the state's assistant attorney general, until 1969. When a vacancy opened up in the Arizona Senate, Governor Jack Williams appointed her to the seat; O'Connor then ran for, and won, reelection the following year.

In 1974, she ran for the position of judge in the Maricopa County Superior Court, winning the race. She served until 1979, when she was appointed to the Arizona State Court of Appeals.

During the 1980 presidential campaign, Ronald Reagan vowed to appoint the first woman to the Supreme Court; on August 19, 1981, he delivered on his promise, nominating O'Connor to replace Potter Stewart. On September 21, the Senate voted unanimously to confirm, and she became the first female justice on the Supreme Court.

Top: Sandra Day O'Connor and President Ronald Reagan sit at the White House, 1981.

Bottom: Sandra Day O'Connor is sworn in as a Supreme Court Justice by Justice Warren Burger, 1981.

Within her first year on the court, O'Connor received more than 60,000 letters from the public— most were positive, but a few criticized her presence on the male-dominated court. Drawing on the lessons in tenacity she learned as a child on her family's ranch, O'Connor was determined to prove that a woman could thrive in a man's world. She spent 24 years on the court, retiring in 2006 but staying active on the lecture circuit and writing several books. She was awarded the Presidential Medal of Freedom in 2009.

Sandra Day O'Connor (far left) pictured with (left to right) Justices Sonia Sotomayor, Ruth Bader Ginsburg, and Elena Kagan.

Meriwether Lewis 1774–1809

Meriwether Lewis was born in Albemarle County in the Colony of Virginia on August 18, 1774. His father died from pneumonia when he was five years old, and he and his mother then moved to Georgia to live with his mother's new husband. Lewis did not receive a formal education until he was 13 years old, but before then he spent his time hunting and developing outdoorsman skills. At the age of 13, Lewis moved back to Virginia where he began his schooling under private tutors and lived under the guardianship of his father's older brother. Lewis graduated from Liberty Hall (now Washington and Lee University) in 1793 and joined the Virginia Militia that year. He joined the United States Army in 1795, where he rose through the ranks and met William Clark, his soon to-be partner in the Corps of Discovery.

Lewis retired from the army in 1801 and was appointed to the position of secretary to President Thomas Jefferson, whom Lewis knew from a social club in Albemarle County. He lived in the presidential mansion during Jefferson's presidency and socialized with many prominent members of the American government. In 1903, Jefferson made the Louisiana Purchase, expanding the nation's realm of control enormously. Jefferson wanted to know about the region and hoped to establish a water route to the west coast to make trade with Asia easier. Lewis, along with William Clark and their crew of Army personnel, departed from St. Charles, Missouri, on May 16, 1804. They reached the Pacific Ocean by November of 1805, wintered in Oregon, and then returned in 1806 with a vast array of biological specimens and information of an overland route to the Pacific.

Lewis was granted the governorship of the Louisiana Territory and settled in St. Louis when he returned. He made plans to publish the documents of the Corps of Discovery's expedition but had difficulty completing his writing. As governor of the territory, he promoted the fur trade and resolved tensions between warring Native American tribes. He wanted to protect Native Americans from settlers encroaching on their lands with treaties, but he was not very successful in the endeavor. Merriwether Lewis died on October 11, 1809, at an inn southeast of Nashville, Tennessee. He died from two gunshot wounds, one to the head and one to the gut, and it is not known whether he commited suicide or whether he was murdered.

Meriwether Lewis was an explorer who led the Corps of Discovery on the first transcontinental journey across the United States.

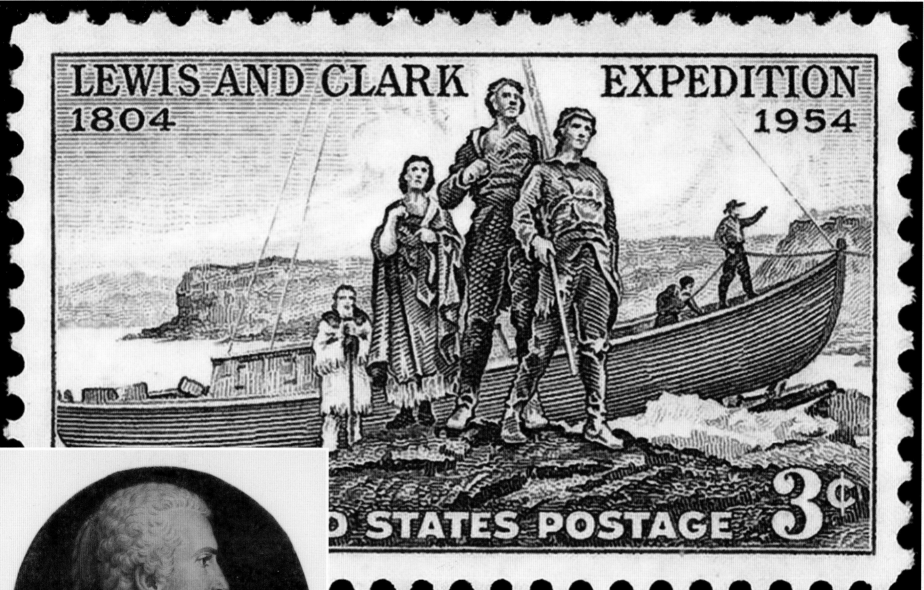

LEWIS AND CLARK EXPEDITION
1804   1954

UNITED STATES POSTAGE   3¢

Top: The Lewis and Clark Expedition happened twelve years after Sir Alexander Mackenzie's transcontinental exploration of Canada.

Left: Merriwether Lewis was a Freemason who petitioned the Grand Lodge in Pennsylvania for a new lodge to be created in St. Louis, where Lewis served as the Master of the lodge when it was established.

William Clark 1770–1838

William Clark was born in Caroline County in the Colony of Virginia on August 1, 1770. He was the ninth child of John and Ann Rogers Clark, who were Virginia natives with possible English and Scottish heritage. His five older brothers all fought during the Revolutionary War, and after the war, his eldest brothers arranged for the family to move to Kentucky. They settled on a plantation near Louisville, Kentucky, in 1785, where William would spend much of his young adulthood until 1803. William was home schooled as a child and was somewhat embarrassed by his makeshift education, although he learned many practical outdoorsman skills from his oldest brother. In 1790, at 19 years of age, William volunteered in the local militia to fight in the Northwest Indian Wars.

William served on many expeditions and fought in many skirmishes against Native Americans, but his time in the military was limited. He retired in 1796 due to poor health and returned to his family's plantation in Kentucky. In 1803, William was recruited by Meriwether Lewis to co-command the Corps of Discovery's expedition west into America's new territory. Their mission was to establish trade with Native Americans, find a water passage to the Pacific Ocean, and establish U.S. sovereignty in the territory. To William and Meriwether's surprise, they found that many of the Native American tribes and bands in the West had already established trade with European groups.

Although Clark was denied the rank of captain on the expedition by the Senate, despite the insistence of both Meriwether Lewis and President Jefferson, Clark assumed equal authority during their journey west. He took charge of surveying and drawing maps of the regions, managing the expedition's supplies, and coordinating hunts for food. Upon their return, Clark was appointed the position of brigadier general of the Louisiana Territory's militia as well an Indian Agent. Clark settled in St. Louis, Missouri, married and had five children, and continued his work as an Indian Agent promoting Jeffersonian ideals of American expansionism. He died on September 1, 1838, and is buried at Bellefontaine Cemetery in St. Louis, Missouri.

William Clark co-commanded the Corps of Discovery's expedition west to explore the newly acquired Louisiana Territory at the beginning of the nineteenth century. After the expedition he served as an Indian Agent and eventually as the Superintendent of Indian Affairs.

Top: Spanish authorities in New Spain learned of the expedition's goal of reaching the Pacific Ocean in Spanish territory. The Spanish sent four militias to intercept the Corps of Discovery, but the expeditions missed the Corps of Discovery in Nebraska and were never able to catch up with them. The Corps of Discovery covered nearly 70 to 80 miles a day.

Left: William Clark was an Indian Agent who believed that assimilation was the best option for Native Americans to cope with white settlement, but despite his beliefs, the Bureau of Indian Affairs ordered several relocations of Native Americans to reservations under Clark's command.

Sacajawea 1788–1812, 1884?

Meriwether Lewis and William Clark were recruited by President Thomas Jefferson to explore the upper reaches of the Missouri River. Their job was to find the most direct route to the Pacific Ocean—the legendary Northwest Passage. Setting out in 1803, they worked their way up the Missouri River and then stopped for the winter to build a fort near a trading post in present-day North Dakota. This is where they met the pregnant Shoshone teenager known as Sacajawea.

Actually, they met her through her husband, Toussaint Charbonneau. He was a French fur trader who lived with the Shoshone (he is said to have purchased Sacajawea from members of another group who had captured her, so it may be inaccurate to call her his "wife"). Although Sacajawea is credited with guiding Lewis and Clark's expedition to the Pacific, the only reason she (and her newborn baby) went along at all was that her husband had been hired as a translator.

The only facts known about Sacajawea come from the journals of Lewis and Clark's expedition team. According to these, we know that she did not translate for the group—with the exception of a few occasions when they encountered other Shoshone. But because she did not speak English, she served as more of a go-between for her husband, the explorers, and members of other tribes they encountered in their travels. Concerning her knowledge of a route to the Pacific, Lewis and Clark knew far more about the land than she did. Only when they reached the area occupied by her own people was she able to point out a few landmarks, but they were not of any great help.

Top: The myth of Sacajawea as the Native American princess who pointed the way to the Pacific was created and perpetuated by the many books and movies that romanticized her story.

Right: In 2000, she was given the U.S. Mint's ultimate honor when it released the Sacajawea Golden Dollar. At the same time, though, the Mint's website incorrectly states that she "guided the adventurers from the Northern Great Plains to the Pacific Ocean and back."

Over time, Sacajawea has evolved to serve as a symbol of friendly relations between the U.S. government and Native Americans.

This isn't to say that she did not make important contributions to the journey's success. Journals note that Sacajawea was a great help to the team when she took it upon herself to rescue essential medicines and supplies that had been washed into a river. Her knowledge of edible roots and plants was invaluable when game and other sources of food were hard to come by. Most important, Sacajawea served as a sort of human peace symbol. Her presence reassured the various Native American groups who encountered Lewis and Clark that the explorers' intentions were peaceful. No Native American woman, especially one with a baby on her back, would have been part of a war party.

There are two very different accounts of Sacajawea's death. Although some historical documents say she died in South Dakota in 1812, Shoshone oral tradition claims she lived until 1884 and died in Wyoming. Regardless of differing interpretations of her life and death, Sacajawea will always be a heroine of American history.

Kit Carson 1809–1868

Christopher Houston "Kit" Carson became a legend in his own time, living long enough to see his frontier adventures reinvented in dime novels. Raised in Missouri, he was apprenticed as a teenager to a saddlemaker. Feeling restless, he defiantly left home in 1826 and was hired on as a herder with a caravan bound for Santa Fe. The saddlers offered a reward of one penny for his return.

From Santa Fe he ventured to Taos. The young adventurer fell in love with the locale and made Taos his home base for the rest of his life. For the next several years, Carson ranged throughout the Rockies working as a fur trapper. He learned Native American customs and languages, but he also fought on numerous occasions against hostile warriors. From 1829 through 1864, he engaged in approximately 30 skirmishes and battles against warriors from various tribes.

The rendezvous of 1835 proved unusually eventful for Carson. He shot a bullying trapper named Shunar in a mounted duel. He also traded for his first wife, a beautiful Arapaho maiden named Waanike, who gave birth to two children. Sadly, Waanike died of illness around 1838. In 1842 Carson was hired as a guide for $100 a month by Lieutenant John C. Frémont. Over the next four years, Carson accompanied Frémont as guide and hunter on three explorations across much of the West. Assigned to carry dispatches to Washington, D.C., Carson reached the nation's capital to find that he had become famous.

Back in New Mexico he was appointed an American Indian agent, and he served honestly and well for a decade. Many reservation American Indians called him "Father Kit." During the Civil War he became lieutenant colonel of the First New Mexico Volunteer Infantry. By 1864 Carson was a brigadier general, and he commanded a punitive expedition into the Texas panhandle. During the ensuing Battle of Adobe Walls, Colonel Carson dueled 2,000 warriors—more than any other commander until George Armstrong Custer in 1876. Carson married Josefa Jaramillo in 1843, but she died in 1868 following the birth of their seventh child. Bereaved and in bad health, Carson died a month later.

Kit Carson was an explorer, frontiersman, fur trapper, and Indian Agent who became an icon of the West. Kit Carson became the courageous character of many dime novels at the time that showcased Kit's ingenuity, tenacity, and sense of adventure.

Top: The last known photo of Kit Carson in Boston during a trip he made with Ute and Ouray chiefs in 1868 two months before his death.

Left: Possibly the first photo ever taken of Kit Carson. Kit was an early American settler of the southwest, living in New Mexico well before it became a part of American territory.

John C. Frémont 1813–1890

Allan Nevins, the most noted of John C. Frémont's biographers, entitled his two-volume study *Frémont, the West's Greatest Adventurer*. Frémont lived up to this label during his years as a daring explorer, exhibiting courage and endurance to a heroic degree. Frémont was personable and handsome, with an aptitude for attracting benefactors—including one who provided a college education and another who arranged a commission with the U.S. Topographical Corps.

On wilderness expeditions with the Corps, Frémont acquired expert training and a taste for exploration. Lieutenant Frémont impressed Missouri Senator Thomas Hart Benton, a powerful spokesperson for westward expansion. Another member of the family who aided his career was Benton's remarkable daughter, Jessie. When Frémont returned from an 1841 expedition into Iowa Territory, he married Jessie. She eventually bore him five children, worked behind the scenes on his behalf, and provided him with publicity and financial support via her literary efforts. Senator Benton and others interested in the American acquisition of the Oregon country obtained authorization for an 1842 expedition along the Oregon Trail. The incomparable scout Kit Carson guided the party of 26 people, which was commanded by Frémont. An account of this adventure, prepared by husband and wife, excited the public and made John C. Frémont a household name.

Prompted by Benton, Congress authorized a second and far more extensive exploration. Frémont, Carson, and 40 others were gone for more than a year, journeying to Oregon, California, the Great Salt Lake, and Santa Fe. By the time Frémont returned to St. Louis in 1844, expansionist James K. Polk was conducting a successful presidential campaign. In 1845 President Polk sent Frémont, again guided by Carson, back to California. When Frémont arrived, the Mexican War had begun, and the expedition fought in several California Skirmishes. In 1856 Frémont made a good showing as the first presidential candidate of the newly organized Republican Party (he was defeated by James Buchanan). During the Civil War Frémont was appointed a major general, but military controversies caused his resignation. The aging hero returned to the West as territorial governor of Arizona from 1878 through 1883.

John C. Frémont was an explorer and politician who led five expeditions into the American West in the 1840s. He was the first presidential candidate for the Republican party in 1856.

Top: An illustration of Frémont climbing the 13,000 foot peak that is now called Frémont Peak during his first expedition that explored the Rocky Mountains. The mountain is the third highest peak in Wyoming.

Bottom: John C. Frémont (seated) with Kit Carson. Carson served as Frémont's guide in the West, exploring the Rocky Mountains, the region around the Great Salt Lake, Oregon Country, and the Sierra Nevada Mountains in California.

John Wesley Powell 1834–1902

Captain John Wesley Powell, future explorer of the Colorado River, commanded a Union artillery battery during the Battle of Shiloh. When he raised his arm to signal his battery to fire, a Confederate bullet shattered his elbow. His right forearm was amputated, but he returned to action and earned promotion to major. The oldest son of a Methodist minister, Powell had been a teacher since the age of 18. After the war, Major Powell was a college lecturer and museum curator who led extended field trips into the Rocky Mountains.

There had been previous surveys of the Colorado River, but 150 perilous miles remained unexplored. Major Powell secured donations, supervised the construction of three heavy boats, and enlisted 11 people. The 1869 expedition overcame furious currents and treacherous rapids in the Grand Canyon. One boat was shattered, supplies were lost, and three people deserted and were then killed by hostile warriors.

The one-armed Powell rode horseback, helped muscle boats through the rapids of the Colorado River, and clambered up the steep walls of the Grand Canyon. Powell and his surviving members emerged to public acclaim, which he expanded with a lecture tour. He organized another Colorado River expedition in 1871, then other trips to other rugged locales. Powell was appointed director of the U.S. Geological Survey in 1881, a position he held with distinction for 14 years.

John Wesley Powell was an explorer, geologist, and educator who explored the Green and Colorado Rivers in the American Southwest, leading the first government exploration of the Grand Canyon.

Top: The first Powell Geographic Expedition led by John Wesley Powell camping along the Green River in Wyoming.

Bottom: Here John Wesley Powell is seen with the headman of the Southern Paiute near the Virgin River in southern Utah. John Wesley Powell later became the first director of the Bureau of Ethnology at the Smithsonian Institute.

Amelia Earheart 1897–1937

Amelia Earhart was born in Atchison, Kansas, in 1897. From a young age, Earhart's mother encouraged young Amelia's sense of adventure. She spent much of her time playing outside, collecting bugs, and hunting rats. Throughout her childhood, she compiled a scrapbook of newspaper clippings on women in male-oriented fields. Earhart was homeschooled with her sister until the family moved to Des Moines, Iowa, and the children enrolled in public school.

The family relocated to Minnesota, Missouri, and finally Chicago, where Earhart finished her senior year of high school. After briefly attending college in Pennsylvania, Earhart moved to Toronto and served as a nurse to soldiers during World War I. She then moved to California to live with her parents.

In 1920, Earhart took a 10-minute plane ride while visiting an airfield, and she decided that she wanted to learn how to fly. She saved up $1,000 for flying lessons, and eventually bought her own biplane. She was the 16th woman in the U.S. to be issued a pilot's license.

In the 1920s, Earhart's family lost their money, and her parents got divorced. She moved to Boston with her mother and found employment as a teacher and a social worker. While in Massachusetts, Earhart continued to show an interest in flying, becoming the vice president of the American Aeronautical Society's Boston Chapter and investing in a local airport, which she also flew out of.

In 1928, Earhart got an offer to be the first woman to fly across the Atlantic Ocean. Wilmer Stultz acted as the pilot and Louis Gordon the copilot on the 20-hour trip, and Earhart kept a flight log. Stultz, Gordon, and Earhart were celebrated as heroes upon their return to the United States, and Earhart eventually gained celebrity status.

Top: Amelia Earhart was the first woman to fly solo across the Atlantic Ocean. She was also an aeronautical engineer, a member of the National Woman's Party, and supporter of the Equal Rights Amendment.

Bottom: Amelia Earhart talking with Fred Noonan, who served as Amelia's second navigator during her first attempt to fly around the world.

Amelia Earhart has posthumously been honored in a number of ways, including a number of buildings and ships named after her and inductions into the National Aviation Hall of Fame and National Women's Hall of Fame.

In 1932, Earhart became the first woman to fly solo nonstop across the Atlantic Ocean. She continued making solo flights to and from different destinations, and set seven women's aviation records between 1930 and 1935. In 1937, Earhart began the first around-the-world-flight at the equator. After completing over 22,000 miles of her flight, she and her navigator vanished. A search effort went on for weeks, but Earhart and her navigator were never found.

Bessie Coleman 1892–1926

Born in Atlanta, Texas, on January 26, 1892, Bessie Coleman and her family moved to Waxahachie when she was two. At six she began attending school, walking four miles every day to reach a segregated, one-room schoolhouse, where she excelled at reading and math. Her schooling was interrupted each year by the cotton harvest, which she was required to take part in. By age twelve, Coleman began attending the Missionary Baptist Church School. As a young adult she attended the Oklahoma Colored Agriculture and Normal University (now Langston University).

In 1916, Coleman moved to Chicago, Illinois, where she worked as a manicurist in a barbershop. When she heard stories from the World War I pilots frequenting the shop, Coleman knew she wanted to fly. But as a woman and the daughter of an African-American mother and a mostly Cherokee father, she was denied entry to American flight schools. Coleman took a proactive approach: She took classes in French, then moved to Paris, where she learned to fly.

Coleman became the first woman of African-American and Native American descent to earn a pilot's license and an international aviation license. She returned to the U.S. and became a hugely popular stunt flyer and parachutist, admired by people of all races for her daring aerial maneuvers. Sadly, Coleman died at the young age of 34, after an accident during a stunt rehearsal. She was inducted into the National Aviation Hall of Fame in 2006, still an inspiration to women in aviation.

Bessie Coleman was an aviator and stunt pilot who was the first African-American woman and first person of Native American descent to attain a pilot license.

Top: Bessie Coleman pictured circa 1922.

Right: Bessie Coleman has been inducted into the National Women's Hall of Fame and the National Aviation Hall of Fame. A library in Chicago is named after her as well as street names in many of the nation's airports.

Sally Ride 1951–2012

Sally Kristen Ride was born on May 26, 1951, in Los Angeles, California, where she attended the Westlake School for Girls on a scholarship and was a nationally ranked tennis player. But science was her first love, and she earned bachelor's degrees in both English and physics from Stanford University, then a master's degree and a PhD in physics.

In 1978, the same year she received her PhD, Ride applied to join NASA's astronaut program, and beat out 1,000 other hopefuls for a spot. She began her NASA career as a ground-based flight controller, but in 1983, after undergoing rigorous training, Ride got her chance to go into space. Brushing off sexist questions and comments from the media, Ride's only concern was to perform her job as best she could; and on June 18, 1983, she became the first American woman to go to space, as a member of the *Challenger* crew.

Ride travelled to space again in 1984, and was scheduled for a third trip; sadly, the Challenger disaster on January 28, 1986, grounded her permanently. She served on the commission that investigated the space shuttle explosion, and later served on the commission that investigated the *Columbia* disaster—the only person to serve on both panels.

After NASA, Ride became the director of the California Space Institute at the University of California, San Diego, and taught physics at the school. In 2001, she founded Sally Ride Science, a company that creates educational products to inspire young people interested in STEM (science, technology, engineering, math) careers, focusing especially on girls.

Although Ride passed away in 2012 after a battle with pancreatic cancer, her legacy continues to inspire. She has received numerous awards and honors, including the National Space Society's von Braun Award and the Lindbergh Eagle Award, and inductions into the National Women's Hall of Fame and the Astronaut Hall of Fame. While women in STEM careers make up less than 25 percent of those who pursue them, the numbers continue to grow—thanks in part to groundbreaking women like Sally Ride.

Sally Ride became the first American woman in space during NASA's 1983 *Challenger* mission. She later taught physics and optics at the University of California, San Diego and served on the committee that investigated the 1986 *Challenger* and 2003 *Columbia* space-shuttle disasters.

Top: A photo of Sally Ride on June 18, 1983, on the flight deck of the space shuttle *Challenger*.

Right: Sally Ride pictured with the Challenger crew. The Challenger mission was the first mission to launch a five-member crew into space. The mission also made Ride the first American female to go into space.

George Catlin 1796–1872

Mesmerized by Native Americans, George Catlin became the first artist of consequence to record western tribal groups and their way of life. His mother had been captured by Native Americans as a little girl, and he grew up hearing exciting tales of frontier adventures. Catlin briefly practiced law, but he soon yielded to his passion for art. Teaching himself to paint, he moved to Philadelphia to establish himself as a portrait artist. In 1824 Catlin encountered a group of 15 western chieftains on a tour of the East, and he resolved to preserve on canvas the Native Americans of the West before they became "corrupted by civilization."

The artist journeyed to St. Louis and gained the support of famed explorer William Clark, who was Superintendent of Indian Affairs for the vast western region acquired through the Louisiana Purchase. Catlin accompanied Clark to treaty councils, then traveled to Fort Leavenworth, Fort Laramie, and perhaps as far as the Great Salt Lake. In 1832 Catlin boarded the American Fur Company's new steamboat, *Yellow Stone*, for a trip up the Missouri to western trading posts. As he came across new tribes, he sketched and painted rapidly, producing as many as six works in a single day. He carefully produced portraits with intricate details of dress, equipment, decoration, and hairstyle, but he used broad strokes for the backgrounds, which could be filled in later. He also recorded village scenes, religious ceremonies, and domestic activities. Sensing his genuine admiration, the tribe members readily accepted "the great medicine painter."

In six years Catlin produced more than 600 scenes and portraits of 48 tribal groups. It was a timely endeavor, because smallpox and other diseases, along with warfare with the Europeans, had already taken a terrible toll on the tribes. The way of life Catlin recorded would soon vanish. Although he was not a technically accomplished artist, the exotic nature of his subject matter exerted a magnetic appeal on the public.

A portrait of George Catlin at the age of 28.

George Catlin was an explorer and artist who travelled to the West five times in the 1830s and depicted various Native American tribes in his art.

A painting by George Catlin of Chief Buffalo Bull's Back Fat, or Stu-mick-o-súcks.

Zebulon Pike 1779–1813

Almost overlooked in the wake of the Lewis and Clark adventure is the probe by Captain Zebulon Montgomery Pike into the unexplored southwestern reaches of the Louisiana Purchase. Pike had been in the army since the age of 15, when he joined his father's command as a cadet. He served at several frontier outposts, married the daughter of a general, and, in 1805, he led an exploration to the headwaters of the Mississippi River.

The next year Pike left St. Louis, taking about 20 comrades toward the Rockies. The party erected a stockade at present-day Pueblo, Colorado, and then partially ascended the peak that now bears Pike's name. After exploring the Royal Gorge early in 1807, Pike and his group were arrested for crossing into Spanish territory. An escort marched them to Santa Fe for questioning, and later across Texas—inadvertently providing more data—before depositing the Americans in Louisiana. Pike was promoted to major in 1808, then to brigadier general during the War of 1812. General Pike was killed in action at the age of 34.

1. Dearborn. 3. Jackson. 5. Brown.
2. Scott. 4. Harrison. 6. Pike.

AMERICAN GENERALS.

Zebulon Pike illustrated here along with five other generals from the War of 1812. Pike is pictured on the bottom right. Andrew Jackson is featured at the top of the illustration.